Bread-Free Bread

Bread-Free
Bread

Gluten-Free, Grain-Free, Amazingly Healthy Veggie- and Seed-Based Recipes

NERISSA ODEN

THE COUNTRYMAN PRESS · WOODSTOCK, VT.

Published by The Countryman Press,
P.O. Box 748, Woodstock, VT 05091
Distributed by W. W. Norton & Company, Inc.,
500 Fifth Avenue, New York, NY 10110
Printed in the United States

Bread-Free Bread
ISBN 978-1-58157-280-3

10 9 8 7 6 5 4 3 2 1

To my husband, Joe Vitale,
who encouraged me to share my creativity with others in a HUGE way.
You ate every version of bread I made with eager enjoyment.
Your dislike of plain vegetables coupled with avoidance of your food sensitivities
and high carbohydrate foods, challenged me in new ways and helped
to shape what is now called *Bread-Free Bread.*
I am grateful for you. Your love, encouragement and support seed miracles!
I love you.

CONTENTS

What Is Bread-Free Bread?

Sandwich Breads

Quick Breads & Muffins

Crackers & Biscuits

Tortillas

Cookies, Cakes & Bars

Appendix

Beyond Bread

My vision for a bread-free bread world

Imagine a near future world where your bread has been freed from the bonds of tradition. In this world most breads are made almost entirely from leafy vegetables, fruits, nuts, and seeds. Bread-free bread options would exist in every restaurant, fast-food chain, and grocery store.

People would stop buying traditional flours made from the dehydrating and grinding of wheat and would go directly from the produce aisle to the kitchen.

I imagine a world where people feel empowered in their kitchen to turn nutrient-rich vegetables into breads that nourish them and their children. I imagine a feeling of independence regained. They would no longer be limited by their eat-on-the-run options. People everywhere would be using vegetables, seeds, and nuts, along with their own creativity, to make convenience food that they love and that keeps them and their family healthy.

What a beautiful world that would be!

What Is Bread-Free Bread?

A previously unknown way to make "breads" from fresh vegetables and seeds, using common tools from the average kitchen.

While exploring bread, its ingredients and mass appeal, I came to a couple of conclusions about the way I was making bread. First, bread-free bread is *not* a traditional bread, and some may say it's not bread at all, because historically breads are made from flour and water. The definition of bread is strictly limited to flour, flour meal, and water. Here is *Merriam-Webster*'s definition of *bread*: (1) "a baked food made from a mixture of flour and water," and (2) "a usually baked and leavened food made of a mixture whose basic constituent is flour or meal."

You, like me, may question this simple and extremely limited definition when we have experienced unlimited varieties of breads in just our lifetime. Think about the long list of breads in your history: yeast rolls, fruit bread, flatbread, quick bread, corn bread, pancakes, tortillas, muffins, biscuits, not to mention tall, short, chewy, fluffy, dark, light, and so on. Yet, they are all mainly composed of these ingredients: flour or meal, water, and yeast. Even potato and corn breads contain mainly wheat flour. All flavorings, herbs, and fruits that we have enjoyed in our breads are tiny in volume when compared to the volume of wheat flour in bread.

What is flour? Historically, flour has been made from wheat and other grains. But should we assume this? What is *flour* exactly? *Merriam-Webster*'s defines *flour* this way:

(1) powder made from a grain (especially wheat) that is used in cooking for making bread, cakes, etc.; (2) a product consisting of finely milled wheat; *also* : a similar product made from another grain or food product (as dried potatoes or fish); (3) a fine soft powder.

Here's where we gain a bit more wriggle room when defining what bread is. The "fine soft powder" used to make bread . . . could be made from anything! Anything that can be dried and ground into a powder, that is. This makes sense as many alternative breads today are made from dehydrated ground roots, seeds, nuts, beans, and gluten-free grains.

Now that our definition of *flour* has been expanded, I'd like to point out that working with any traditional flour can be extremely messy, requiring much cleanup effort. When I made flour breads as research, I was horrified to find a layer of fine food dust covering all items in a four-foot radius, including my floor and rugs. Most would agree that the dehydrating and grinding of flours should best be performed outside the home. Anyone making homemade bread today will need to purchase flour products and expect a messy result. That's why people just purchase bread that's already baked, and leave the mixing and baking to industry.

So what's bread-free bread? Read on.

1. **Bread-free bread is a *baked form* of raw bread.**

   The raw food movement creates traditional foods using only raw ingredients that remain raw and never get cooked. Raw foods do not use flours or grains unless they are prepared by soaking, for the most part. To mimic traditional wheat-based foods, such as pie crusts, crackers, and breads, the raw food movement utilizes two things (1) sticky ingredients that will hold foods together, such as flaxseeds; and (2) dehydrators that dry foods out with fans and very low heat. Raw crackers that are 'baked' in dehydrators over several hours, even days, are crunchy with similar textures to traditional baked crackers. They also handle well and store easily, too.

   Raw food enthusiasts embrace a large variety and amount of nuts, enjoy raw dairy products, avoid highly processed foods, and avoid genetically engineered modified foods. If they so desired they could eat beef tartare (raw ground beef) and ceviche, which is fish that has been "cooked" without heat. In general, they eat very few things that look or act like traditional breads.

2. **Bread-free bread is a *new level* of the Paleo diet.**

   Paleo followers eat only items that can be found and gathered in the environment, such as animals, insects, eggs, fruits, vegetables, nuts and seeds.

   They avoid highly processed foods—including oils, sugars, and flours—as well as farmed foods, such as dairy and grains. Paleo dieters eat very few items that look and act like traditional breads.

3. **Bread-free bread can also be referred to as a quick bread, which is a baked good leavened by baking soda or baking powder instead of yeast.**

4. **Bread-free bread can be called a flatbread because most are baked thin and flat.**

5. **Bread-free bread can also be called a cake, muffin, or biscuit as it may mimic the shape, form, and texture of traditional cakes, muffins, or biscuits.**

6. **Bread-free bread can also be called fruit bread if made with fruit.**

So, what *is* bread-free bread? The simplest answer is, "Bread that is made with nontraditional ingredients, but that looks and acts like bread."

Why Is Bread-Free Bread Healthier Than Other Breads?

Practically all other alternative breads are composed mainly of high-carbohydrate grains, such as rice; highly refined alternative starches such as tapioca flour; allergens, such as palm and nuts; and syrups or questionable sweeteners.

Although our understanding of what it means to be healthy has common characteristics that apply to everyone, health is individual as well. Our genetic markers are passed from one generation to the next, yet are influenced by our individual environments: factors such as air, water, toxic surfaces, toxic products, and food. I would argue that our health is impacted by our food environment the most. Our food environments encompass not only food ingredients and quality, but also water quality, supplements, and medicines. Our health not only comprises nutrients and toxicants but also is greatly influenced by *how* our body interacts with those nutrients and toxicants. Bread-free bread is healthy because it:

- does *not* contain modern bread's chemical ingredients, such as dough conditioners, preservatives, or artificial flavorings and colorings.

- does *not* contain high-carbohydrate flours that are linked to blood sugar spiking, which is linked to many diseases common in the United States, including heart disease, diabetes, and dementia. Even popular alternative breads often contain high-carbohydrate flours such as potato, rice, arrowroot, and tapioca.

- does *not* contain gluten, which is best known as an irritant in celiac disease but also affects far more people as a sensitivity, including intolerances to gluten as well. Gluten is a natural component of most grains that are used in bread. Gluten has also been altered so much by commercial agriculture that experts argue the protein is a new protein previously unknown to man— and to man's digestive tract. Gluten can also be highly processed and turned into its own product that is then used in a huge variety of food products, including ice cream and chewing gum, and no longer limited to bread products.

- does *not* contain the chemical azodicarbonamide, most commonly referred to as the yoga mat chemical because it's used in the manufacturing of yoga mats to give them that air-bubbly cushion. Azodicarbonamide is neither a food nor a food product but is allowed to be used in food products sold in the United States and is used primarily in the making of breads. When azodicarbonamide is baked, it breaks down into the chemical compounds semicarbazide and urethane, which may pose toxic risks of their own.

- does *not* contain most common food allergens in the United States. Food allergens and especially undiagnosed food sensitivities are linked to such autoimmune diseases as Crohn's disease, Graves' disease, rheumatoid arthritis, fibromyalgia, and more.

- includes unprocessed dietary fiber from plants, which is considered healthy to the vast majority of people. Unprocessed high fiber is good on many levels: (1) fiber is needed to move food through our intestinal tract—it's like our conveyer belt; (2) while traveling through our intestines, good micro flora (probiotics) thrive in the high-fiber environment; and (3) bad bacteria and toxins are more easily and thoroughly eliminated if one eats a high-fiber diet.

- contains densely-packed nutrients from whole fresh foods, bringing a sense of satisfaction that lasts longer, with fewer feelings of hunger between meals. This is especially true of breads made from high-nutrient foods, such as kale.

- has more flavor, so adults as well as children find it easier to consume and desire to eat it again.

- is more filling than regular breads, causing most people to eat smaller meals. Maintaining energy between meals is a benefit which is often cited by those who eat bread-free bread.

- gives the bread maker control of the ingredients. The bread maker could choose organic fresh vegetables, fruits, and herbs, as well as gluten-free ingredients, such as gluten-free baking powder.

- leaves the bread maker free to make substitutions that fit individual health preferences. For example, lemon juice can be used instead of vinegar, or fresh eggs could be replaced with a variety of egg substitutes.

The Desire That Created Bread-Free Bread

How did an ordinary girl whose only previous professional experience with food was as a worker in the fast-food industry for six years, get the idea to make alternative breads from nothing but fresh food and seeds?

Living below the poverty line, I grew up on starch-based meals at home, the cheapest food available in high school, and all the fast food I could eat as soon as I was old enough to work in their restaurants. I continued this diet through my twenties and thirties as I worked my way through college, then as a professional editor in film and video. By the time I was 34 years old I was often unable to work because I was sick in bed. I suffered from mold allergies, several seasonal allergies, frequent headaches and migraines, hot flashes, swollen ankles, shortness of breath, adrenal fatigue, exercise exhaustion, chronic sinus drip, heavy sneezing, frequent sore throat, poor concentration, depression, irritability, anxiety, tinnitus, racing heart episodes, and painful periods. I took huge amounts of over-the-counter medications for most of my life, as my focus was only about relieving the discomfort of my ailments.

As I neared my 40th birthday my doctor put me on heavy antibiotics and steroids to help me kick a severe cold that I had had for weeks. This protocol was needed for several weeks before the symptoms subsided. My doctor had no idea how to prevent a similar illness in my future. A friend who is a chiropractor and nutritionist suggested I get tested for food sensitivities, which are also known as delayed food allergies

because they can manifest hours or days later. I took the test, avoided the foods I was shown to be sensitive to, and that's when I got better. I felt like I was 19 again, with extra energy to burn.

I began cooking from scratch with organic ingredients. I ate more raw fresh ingredients, too. My bread, cracker, and chip selections at grocery stores had withered to a handful of choices due to my sensitivity to yeasts and dairy. It was a difficult adjustment. Sunflower seed butter and organic deli meats wrapped in three-ingredient tortillas, or on simple ingredient crackers that I had found, were what enabled me to maintain my diet and yet continue eating in a similar way to how I had my whole life—convenient finger foods requiring low to no cooking.

My doctor didn't understand how avoiding such foods as broccoli, salmon, sesame, black pepper, dairy, and yeast were helping me, but she was excited to hear that all my chronic health ailments had disappeared practically overnight.

I am forever grateful to my friend Dr. Rick Barrett for testing me for food sensitivities, awakening me to a lifelong ignored reality that food can hurt, and for kick-starting my health food journey. That first food sensitivity test opened my eyes and caused an irreversible paradigm shift in me about food and health.

Yet I must give the lion's share of the credit for my health success to those few bread-related choices that helped me: tortillas and crackers. It was the availability of these products that allowed me to achieve my first dramatic shift in diet. At that time, choices for alternative bread products were extremely limited, unlike today. And yet, I see a need for even more choices. Choices that don't involve refined carbohydrates, or nut flours that rank among the top ten food allergens. Like me, you want healthy alternative breads that won't spike your blood sugar, or scare dinner guests who have nut allergies. I want your transition into a bread-free bread world to be full of abundant, tasty healthy options, options that will work with any diet and lifestyle. That's why I wrote this cookbook.

GO DEEPER

After experiencing my paradigm shift in food and health consciousness, it was normal to share my experience with others. People were fascinated by the details I had noticed over time, concerning the interactivity of my personal health and food. Details like how black pepper made me belch like a frat boy, sugar made my ears ring loudly with tinnitus, and dairy caused sinus headaches two and a half days later.

Some people were so impressed with my boundless energy, weight loss, and stories about what I call food powers, that they got tested for food sensitivities, too. And their ailments also went away once they changed their diets! My husband, Joe, was one of the first to get tested. His test showed a high sensitivity to paprika and dairy. He could eat one or the other and not experience asthma symptoms. But if he ate them together, he would experience asthma symptoms within minutes. We easily concluded that his adult-onset asthma diagnosis was really a combination food allergy. He has avoided foods containing both paprika and dairy ever since, and eventually gave up dairy altogether.

In 2009 I created the website www.foodpowers.com, where I posted interviews with others about their delayed food allergies. During these years I read a lot of articles and scoured professional websites about food allergies and food sensitivities. I had learned that sugars and starches were inherently bad for me due to my chronic sensitivities to baker's and brewer's yeasts. I complained often over the lack of alternative breads and crackers. Sprouted-grain breads made me sick. Gluten-free breads were full of highly refined starches that contribute to spikes in blood sugar and yeast (Candida) overgrowth. Paleo breads are exciting, but they more often than not seem like corn bread than like traditional sandwich bread. Also, Paleo breads are most often made from coconut flour and almond meal. If I eat almonds and other nuts often, then I can become sensitive to them and at that point they are no longer healthy for me.

I expanded my ability to cook from scratch. I cooked around my food sensitivities and those of my husband. Because most popular alternative breads weren't good options for me or my husband, I often felt locked out of quick and convenient meals and snacks, such as sandwiches, crackers, cookies, and tortillas. Additionally, my husband disliked most

husband (and everyone else) ate the vegetables disguised as breads and even asked for more.

I knew I was on to something. Being a citizen advocate for increasing food sensitivity awareness, I knew that millions of people have food allergies and food sensitivities to standard ingredients in bread, such as gluten, wheat, yeast, dairy and nuts. So I started to share a few of my recipes. The result was overwhelming praise. People asked for more including leaders in body building, weight loss, fitness, nutrition, and healthy lifestyles.

vegetable dishes. He never seemed to enjoy them. He just preferred meat protein and the largest percentage of his meals were just that.

Starting with just a desire, then a vision, I began turning vegetables into traditional baked goods. I created hamburger buns using only spinach and seeds. I made sandwich bread out of okra. I made biscuits from squash. To my delight, my

Over the last year, I have been perfecting these innovative recipes so anyone can follow them. Using pictures and clear descriptions, home bakers can make their own bread-free bread—without traditional grains, gluten, yeast, sugar, refined oils, highly refined carbs, or nuts—in their own kitchen using basic kitchen tools.

Challenges to Creation

The inspiration moment, the repeated failures, twists and turns that led to the perfect bread-free bread recipes.

The foremost challenge was getting bread-free bread to act like bread, not like quick breads or dressing. Second, I wanted bread that truly reflected its name. Call me naive, but when I looked for spinach bread recipes, I really wanted bread with

to our neighborhood possum—because even when yeast is surrounded by veggies, it makes me sick. By the way, there's a good probability that you, too, are affected negatively by yeasts, fungus, and molds. And because yeast isn't a necessary ingredient to make breads, I concluded that it was an unnecessary and unwanted ingredient. Next, I found a yeast alternative and made the same recipes to compare them.

WORKING BACKWARD

Traditional bread recipes always start with dry ingredients and then liquid ingredients are added. Making breads from mostly

spinach as the first ingredient, not the last.

Now, to make vegetables act like bread, you must understand why traditional bread acts like bread. So I began baking muffins and quick breads. Then I started to create my own recipes for muffins and quick breads, made from scratch. I wanted to know, would they work without oil? Without eggs? With an egg alternative? Without yeast?

I tried baking with yeast twice, and then fed the results

vegetables required me to turn that concept around. I had to think of what healthy dry ingredients I could add to my liquid puréed veggies.

I eventually became adept at turning any vegetable into bread on the first try. In fact, my first published recipe for veggie bread is still a nonspecific base recipe that is included in this cookbook—for those adventurous, nonconformist chefs out there. With the help of *Austin All Natural* magazine, I gave the world the key to turning veggies into bread—using one's own kitchen!

It became clear that, instead of using one master recipe, I had to create individual kinds of bread. And so, as I continued to play with my base recipe in my kitchen, I wrote down all my combinations.

GOODBYE DEHYDRATOR

With the help of the Krazy Kracker Lady's (Abeba Wright) cookbooks, I had successfully used my large, noisy dehydrator to make raw crackers. In fact, when she shared her first raw bread recipe, I got inspired to make my own baked grain-free breads I had been dreaming about. To create recipes that would appeal to most readers, I couldn't use a dehydrator. Seriously, I am not about to force you to buy what is essentially a large space heater that will also take away productive counter space. My husband tells the same joke to everyone about my dehydrator. Joe will say, "She asks me if I want healthy grain-free crackers, I say 'yes,' then she tells me they'll be ready in twelve hours!" There's a truth to most jokes, which is what makes them funny. A dehydrator requirement for bread-free bread was my first reluctant casualty. Truth be told, I still make raw crackers in my dehydrator, in the winter, in my garage. And I don't ask my husband if wants any until they're ready to eat.

HOW MANY CUPS ARE IN A CARROT?

After sending out my first recipe to a core group of friends, I received feedback that made me realize that I had to conform to the norm and measure each ingredient. I had gotten use to my own style. For example any recipe requiring for "one medium tomato" isn't specific enough apparently because "medium" is a relative concept. Also, my instructions that said, "Flavor to taste," had immediately crippled enough friends into

nonaction. So I caved in reluctantly to rigidity and formality of the recipe-making business and began to measure my herbs and spices instead of eyeballing them.

You may notice that my recipes were built around standard vegetable packaging, such as spinach or baby kale (5 ounces), okra (1 quart), and nopales (12.5 ounces of cactus strips). Other vegetables, such as tomatoes, which are sold by weight had to be diced so that they could be measured. I quickly learned that package ounces do not equal weight ounces. I'm grateful for each mistake as they each bore the fruit of knowledge.

WHAT IS PAN LINING PAPER?

Reynolds Pan Lining Paper has foil on one side and parchment paper on the other. Before Pan Lining Paper, I had tried every way I could think of to grease or oil my pans. All or some of the bread would stick to the pan. I tried wax paper next, and it worked much better than oil, but the wax paper stuck to the bread, sometimes badly. I secretly suspected that some of the wax might be melting into the bread, too. Then a friend suggested using parchment paper, and after the very first use I knew it was the key to making a successful bread, every time, and it made me happy. Just before last Christmas I stumbled upon Pan Lining Paper and bought it. The foil grips the pan—no more sliding paper—as I spread the wet batter across my jelly-roll pans. The parchment side of the Pan Lining Paper removes easily from each bread after baking, and it keeps jelly-roll pans and cookie sheets clean! "Joy to the world!" I sang out loud.

Tools You Will Use

A list of basic kitchen tools to make recipes in this cookbook, with a short description of each.

BLENDER

Most bread-free breads were created with a blender to turn solid foods into liquid. A blender with a tamper tool is preferred but not required. Built-in tampers allow you to push the blender's contents into the blade without worrying about your implement reaching the blade itself and being destroyed. Built-in tamper tools make the blending process faster. If your blender does not have a built-in tamper tool, just stop the blender and push the contents toward the blade while the blender is in the off position. Do this as needed.

SINGLE-SERVE BLENDER, OR IMMERSION STICK BLENDER

These modern blenders are perfect for blending jobs that are too small for a normal size-blender. For example, my microwave recipes that were created to serve just one person work best when blended by a machine, not by hand.

FOOD PROCESSOR

You could use a food processor instead of a blender for most of these recipes. When you do this, the breads will have a more visible texture. A food processor is also great at grinding seeds into meal with varying levels of coarseness. Use a mini food processor to grind a small amount of seeds into meal.

COFFEE/SPICE GRINDER

These affordable handheld grinders are perfect for small jobs. They are fast, durable, and lined with stainless steel. Food processors and blenders are too big for small grinding jobs. As an alternative, you could grind a large amount of seeds into meal to be stored and used later. Just be aware that seed meal doesn't keep fresh as long as whole seeds do when stored.

PAN LINING PAPER, PARCHMENT PAPER, OR NON-STICK BAKING LINER

Each of these items work great but I prefer to use Pan Lining Paper for baking bread-free breads. Parchment paper slides easily, whereas baking liners produce edges drier than the middle. Pan Lining Paper has parchment paper on one side and foil on the other. The foil side grips your baking sheet, minimizing sliding. Without the protection of the Pan Lining Paper the dough often touches the baking pan itself and becomes baked on. With Pan Lining Paper my baking sheets stay clean and just need to cool before being stored or reused.

ANGLED ICING SPATULA

Much faster than using a spatula to level the batter thickness. Speed is important when making these breads.

BAKING SHEET (A.K.A. JELLY-ROLL PAN)

It's a cookie sheet with sides. It makes shaping the batter easier for baking. No spillovers!

COOKIE SHEET

A flat, thin baking sheet with no sides.

LOAF, CAKE, AND PIE PANS

For a handful of recipes I use a couple of other pans worth mentioning here:

- 1.5-quart loaf pan (8½ x 4½ x 2½ inches)

- 8-inch square baking pan

- 9-inch round cake pan

- 8½-inch pie pan

- microwave-proof mug or bowl large enough to hold 20 ounces of liquid

DOUGH WHISK OR BALLOON WHISK

I'd like you to consider buying a dough whisk for under $20. A dough whisk does the same work as a spoon and whisk, but it doesn't trap the dough the way a balloon whisk can, which costs you time. And it's faster to clean. Balloon whisks also work and are preferred for the thinner batters, such as for corn bread and cake.

COOLING RACK

Nothing fancy, just keeps breads above the counter to help them cool and expel moisture. If anyone in your house has food allergies, be sure to wash your rack after each use to avoid cross-contamination.

MEASURING CUPS AND SPOONS

I now own about four sets of measuring spoons, but one set is really all you need. I prefer measuring seed meals in multicup measuring cups that are tall and thin because they provide faster and more accurate measurements. I also own a set of measuring cups with handles to measure liquids and chopped vegetables.

SPATULAS

You will need spatulas to remove your batter from blender containers and bowls. You will also shape the batter when transferring to the baking sheet.

Ingredient Substitutions

Awareness of food allergies and food sensitivities is increasing, so with this in mind, I created this section to foster awareness about ingredient substitutions that are relevant to most of my bread-free bread recipes.

ALMOND MEAL, SUNFLOWER SEED MEAL, AND PUMPKIN SEED MEAL

These three ingredients can be used interchangeably but with these two precautions: (1) Pumpkin seeds have a distinctive flavor that can't be masked easily; and (2) sunflower seeds can easily replace almond meal in recipes but as the amount increases, so should the coarseness of the sunflower seed meal. For example, to substitute sunflower seed meal in either banana bread recipe, don't use a fine grind of sunflower seed meal; use a coarse grind instead. Almond meal and almond flour are interchangeable and both are gluten-free.

FLAXSEED MEAL VS. *GOLDEN* FLAXSEED MEAL

The two types of flaxseed meals can be used interchangeably. The only discernable difference between the two is the color. Using a golden flaxseed meal will keep the bread a lighter color.

It's simple and economical to grind your own flaxseeds. Use a coffee/spice grinder, mini food processor, or personal blender with a dry blade to grind small amounts. For a larger quantity, use a regular-size blender with a dry blade or a food processor. To keep flaxseed meal fresh, grind only as much meal as you need, or store larger quantities in a covered container away from light and heat. Flaxseed meal can be expected to last up to 10 months in a dark, cool pantry, or longer in the freezer.

FLAXSEED MEALS VS. CHIA SEED MEAL (ALSO CALLED CHIA FLOUR AND CHIA POWDER)

These seed meals are *not* interchangeable even though they perform the same function—binding blended veggies or fruits together to form breads. The textures of flaxseed meal and chia seed meal are completely different after being baked. Chia seed meal produces a more spongy, or rubbery bread texture, whereas the flaxseed meals produce a lighter and fluffier bread texture. Additionally, chia seeds are much harder than flaxseeds and are more difficult to grind into a powder form, which is why chia seed meal products have varying gritty textures when touched. Because of this, chia seed meals often require much longer exposure times to liquids, to soften them, before they can be baked.

VINEGARS, LEMON JUICE CONCENTRATE, AND LEMON JUICE

These three ingredients can be used interchangeably. I've used all three in my recipes and I never noticed a functional difference between them except in their flavor. In some recipes I do notice a vinegar taste if I have used vinegar.

I used lemon juice concentrate for most recipes because (1) I'm sensitive to vinegar; and (2) it was convenient while I was baking dozens of recipes per week. I recommend that if you have the time, just use fresh lemon juice instead.

The most common vinegars are distilled white, cider, and rice vinegar. I encourage you to have fun experimenting with flavors too, such as raspberry and pear.

EGG WHITES VS. WHOLE EGGS VS. EGG SUBSTITUTES

Egg whites keep my breads airy and light. When bread-free breads are in the blender, a huge amount of tiny bubbles are created and function as air pockets, which survive the baking process. Whole eggs contain yolks, which are fatty. Egg whites contain no fat because they contain no yolks. Yolks impede the creation of air bubbles and shorten bubbles' ability to remain throughout the baking process.

The eggs also act as binding agents. Baking soda and baking powder act as leaveners, which create and increase tiny bubble activity, while the eggs bind those bubbles into place during the baking process.

I use whole eggs when a recipe needs a little fat to give the bread, muffin, or cake the perfect level of moisture and texture. You can separate egg whites from the yolk when using whole eggs, or you can purchase cartons of liquid egg whites.

Some people avoid eggs entirely. In that case, try one of these egg substitutes instead: psyllium husks, guar gum, unflavored gelatin, agar-agar, or a starch-based egg substitute mixture or product.

UNFLAVORED GELATIN VS. AGAR-AGAR POWDER

Every food ingredient is a potential allergen, including unflavored gelatin. Some people have serious allergic reactions when exposed to gelatin, and some have less serious reactions known as food sensitivities. If this sounds like you, then please use agar-agar powder instead. Agar-agar is made from algae and agar-agar powder can be used just like unflavored gelatin. Agar-agar is also suitable for those on a vegan diet.

Bread-Free Bread

SANDWICH BREADS

Lemon Rosemary Squash Bread

MAKES ONE 12 X 17-INCH BREAD

A delicious summer favorite light in color and flavor. Sunflower seeds give this treat a slightly nutty flavor. Perfect for sandwiches and as a complement to soups. Simple tuna fish salad sandwiches will be converted to fine dining. Serve as toast, sandwiches, bite-size snacks, or as the prebaked bottom for your exquisite homemade pizzas.

DRY INGREDIENTS

½ cup raw, shell-free sunflower seeds

2¼ cups golden flaxseed meal

1 tablespoon fresh or dried whole rosemary leaves

1 teaspoon baking soda

1 teaspoon baking powder

½ teaspoon sea salt

WET INGREDIENTS

4 cups chopped fresh yellow summer squash (1 pound squash)

Zest from 1 lemon, plus 2 tablespoons chopped and seeded lemon flesh

½ cup liquid egg whites

1. Preheat the oven to 350°F.

2. Cover a 12 x 17-inch baking sheet with Pan Lining Paper, foil side down.

3. Grind sunflower seeds into a fine meal.

4. In a large bowl, mix together the dry ingredients.

5. Blend wet ingredients thoroughly in blender.

6. Transfer the wet mixture to the bowl of dry ingredients. Mix well and quickly.

7. Scrape the batter onto the prepared baking sheet. Push the mixture to the edges, then level with a spatula. Bake for about 60 minutes or until dry to the touch.

8. Invert bread onto a cooling rack. Remove the pan and paper. Let cool.

9. After cooling, cut into desired pieces or use as a prebaked pizza crust. Store in a sealed container in the refrigerator.

Hippie Chick Bread

MAKES ONE 12 X 17-INCH BREAD

This bread has a delightful mild flavor that appeals to practically everyone.
The light, fresh sunflower flavor reminds one of summer. Hippie Chick Bread
enhances many different traditional sandwich combinations, including
chicken and egg salads, burgers, deli meats, and peanut butter.

DRY INGREDIENTS

1 cup raw, shell-free sunflower seeds

3 cups flaxseed meal

1 teaspoon fresh or dried thyme

1 teaspoon fresh or dried rosemary

1 teaspoon baking soda

1 teaspoon baking powder

1 teaspoon sea salt

WET INGREDIENTS

1 cup chopped tomato

1 cup chopped zucchini

1 cup chopped carrot

1½ cups cooked black beans, or 1 (15 ounce) can, drained and rinsed

½ cup liquid egg whites

2 tablespoons vinegar

1. Preheat the oven to 350°F.

2. Cover a 12 x 17-inch baking sheet with Pan Lining Paper, foil side down.

3. Grind sunflower seeds into a fine meal.

4. In a large bowl, mix together the dry ingredients.

5. Blend wet ingredients thoroughly in blender.

6. Transfer the wet mixture to the bowl of dry ingredients. Mix well and quickly.

7. Scrape the batter onto the prepared baking sheet. Push the mixture to the edges, then level with a spatula. Bake for about 60 minutes or until dry to the touch.

8. Invert bread onto a cooling rack. Remove the pan and paper. Let cool.

9. After cooling, cut into desired pieces or use as a prebaked pizza crust. Store in a sealed container in the refrigerator.

Taste of India Bread

A mild flavor of Middle Eastern spice with garlic as decoration on top.
This bread is complete as a bite-size snack, a side dish, and for sandwiches.
A favorite with lovers of garlic.

DRY INGREDIENTS

1½ cups golden flaxseed meal

½ cup raw pine nuts (2 ounces)

2 teaspoons curry powder

1 teaspoon baking soda

1 teaspoon baking powder

½ teaspoon sea salt

WET INGREDIENTS

1½ cups cooked garbanzo beans, or 1 (15 ounce) can, drained and rinsed

½ cup chopped red bell pepper

¼ cup liquid egg whites

2 tablespoons vinegar

4 to 6 garlic cloves, sliced lengthwise into 4 or 5 slivers each

1. Preheat the oven to 350°F.

2. Cover a 9 x 13-inch baking sheet with Pan Lining Paper, foil side down.

3. Grind the raw pine nuts finely.

4. In a medium bowl, mix together the dry ingredients.

5. Blend wet ingredients (except sliced garlic) thoroughly in blender.

6. Transfer the wet mixture to the bowl of dry ingredients. Mix well and quickly.

7. Scrape the batter onto the prepared baking sheet. Push the mixture to the edges, then level with a spatula. Top with garlic slices and bake for about 60 minutes or until dry to the touch.

8. Place upside down on a cooling rack. Remove the pan and paper. Let cool.

9. After cooling, cut into desired pieces or use as a prebaked pizza crust. Store in a sealed container in the refrigerator.

Southern Flame Bread

MAKES ONE 12 X 17-INCH BREAD

Adult flavor for adults. Made mostly from kale, this bread has the right amount of spicy hotness. Chipotle powder gives it warmth, while a serrano pepper adds the heat. Tasty, nutritious, and filling, kale bread can keep you going all day with steady energy or just reduce that hungry feeling between meals. Eat the bread plain, as toast, sandwiches, bite-size snacks, or as the prebaked bottom for all your homemade pizzas.

DRY INGREDIENTS

1 cup raw, shell-free pumpkin seeds

1½ cups flaxseed meal

1 teaspoon baking soda

½ teaspoon baking powder

½ teaspoon chipotle powder

½ teaspoon sea salt

WET INGREDIENTS

1 cup chopped tomato

1 cup chopped red bell pepper

1 serrano pepper

11 cups fresh baby kale leaves or chopped curly kale (5-6 ounces)

½ cup liquid egg whites

1 tablespoon vinegar

1. Preheat the oven to 350°F.

2. Cover a 12 x 17-inch baking sheet with Pan Lining Paper, foil side down.

3. Grind the pumpkin seeds into a fine meal.

4. In a large bowl, mix together the dry ingredients.

5. Blend wet ingredients thoroughly in blender.

6. Transfer the wet mixture to the bowl of dry ingredients. Mix well and quickly.

7. Scrape the batter onto the prepared baking sheet. Push the mixture to the edges, then level with a spatula. Bake for about 60 minutes or until dry to the touch.

8. Place upside down on a cooling rack. Remove the pan and paper. Let cool.

9. After cooling, cut into desired pieces or use as a prebaked pizza crust. Store in a sealed container in the refrigerator.

Southwestern Okra Bread

MAKES ONE 12 X 17-INCH BREAD

Even people who don't like the feel of okra love this spicy okra bread.
Flavored with southwestern chili powder and cayenne pepper, this flaky bread pleases
everyone. Perfect for sandwiches and snacks.

DRY INGREDIENTS

1 cup raw, shell-free sunflower seeds

1½ cups flaxseed meal

2 tablespoons chili powder

½ teaspoon cayenne pepper

1 teaspoon baking soda

1 teaspoon baking powder

½ teaspoon sea salt

WET INGREDIENTS

3 cups chopped fresh okra (about 8 ounces)

1 cup chopped tomato

½ cup liquid egg whites

1 tablespoon vinegar

3 whole okra pods, sliced lengthwise into 4 or 5 slivers each

1. Preheat the oven to 350°F.

2. Cover a 12 x 17-inch baking sheet with Pan Lining Paper, foil side down.

3. Grind sunflower seeds into a fine meal.

4. In a large bowl, mix together the dry ingredients.

5. Blend wet ingredients (except sliced okra) thoroughly in blender.

6. Transfer the wet mixture to the bowl of dry ingredients. Mix well and quickly.

7. Scrape the batter onto the prepared baking sheet. Push the mixture to the edges, then level with a spatula. Top with okra slices and bake for about 60 minutes or until dry to the touch.

8. Place upside down on a cooling rack. Remove the pan and paper. Let cool.

9. After cooling, cut into desired pieces or use as a prebaked pizza crust. Store in a sealed container in the refrigerator.

Cactus Bread

MAKES ONE 12 X 17-INCH BREAD

Prickly pears, also known as nopales, are a unique, plentiful superfood. Pads, or paddles, from the prickly pear cactus are sold skinned and cut, and have been eaten for thousands of years. Potential health benefits of cactus include weight loss and blood sugar stability. Nopales are also high in fiber.

DRY INGREDIENTS

1 cup raw, shell-free pumpkin seeds

1½ cups flaxseed meal

1 teaspoon ground cumin

1 teaspoon garlic powder

1 teaspoon baking soda

1 teaspoon baking powder

½ teaspoon sea salt

WET INGREDIENTS

3½ cups fresh precut cactus (1 [12.5-ounce] package)

½ serrano pepper

½ cup liquid egg whites

1 tablespoon vinegar

1. Preheat the oven to 350°F.

2. Cover a 12 x 17-inch baking sheet with Pan Lining Paper, foil side down.

3. Grind pumpkin seeds into a fine meal.

4. In a large bowl, mix together the dry ingredients.

5. Blend wet ingredients thoroughly in blender.

6. Transfer the wet mixture to the bowl of dry ingredients. Mix well and quickly.

7. Scrape the batter onto the prepared baking sheet. Push the mixture to the edges, then level with a spatula. Bake for about 60 minutes or until dry to the touch.

8. Place upside down on a cooling rack. Remove the pan and paper. Let cool.

9. After cooling, cut into desired pieces or use as a prebaked pizza crust. Store in a sealed container in the refrigerator.

Holy Hotness Bread

MAKES ONE 9 X 13-INCH BREAD

This spinach bread is tempered with the flavor of red bell pepper and accented
with a generous amount of warmth from serrano pepper. A dark bread
with sinful appeal. Eat the bread plain, as toast, sandwiches, bite-size snacks,
or as the prebaked bottom for all your homemade pizzas.

DRY INGREDIENTS

1½ cups flaxseed meal

½ teaspoon baking soda

½ teaspoon baking powder

¼ teaspoon sea salt

WET INGREDIENTS

⅓ cup chopped tomato

1 serrano pepper

¼ cup chopped red bell pepper

11 cups fresh baby spinach (5-6 ounces)

¼ cup liquid egg whites

1½ teaspoons vinegar

1. Preheat the oven to 350°F.

2. Cover a 9 x 13-inch baking sheet with Pan Lining Paper, foil side down.

3. In a medium bowl, mix together the dry ingredients.

4. Blend wet ingredients thoroughly in blender.

5. Transfer the wet mixture to the bowl of dry ingredients. Mix well and quickly.

6. Scrape the batter onto the prepared baking sheet. Push the mixture to the edges, then level with a spatula. Bake for about 60 minutes or until dry to the touch.

7. Place upside down on a cooling rack. Remove the pan and paper. Let cool.

8. After cooling, cut into desired pieces or use as a prebaked pizza crust. Store in a sealed container in the refrigerator.

Texas Traditional Okra Bread

MAKES ONE 12 X 17-INCH BREAD

They will never guess they ate okra! This hearty bread has great height, making it perfect for big eaters. Full of traditional butter flavor, made possible by KAL brand nutritional yeast. Yeast-sensitive persons can use imitation butter alternatives. Perfect for French toast, but also serve as plain toast, sandwiches, or as a side bread.

DRY INGREDIENTS

1 cup raw, shell-free sunflower seeds

2¼ cups golden flaxseed meal

1 teaspoon baking soda

1 teaspoon baking powder

2 tablespoons KAL nutritional yeast or your favorite imitation butter powder alternative

1 teaspoon sea salt

WET INGREDIENTS

3 cups chopped fresh okra (about 8 ounces)

1 cup chopped tomato

½ cup liquid egg whites

1 tablespoon vinegar

3 whole okra pods, sliced lengthwise into 4 or 5 slivers each

1. Preheat the oven to 350°F.

2. Cover a 12 x 17-inch baking sheet with Pan Lining Paper, foil side down.

3. Grind sunflower seeds into a fine meal.

4. In a large bowl, mix together dry ingredients.

5. Blend wet ingredients (except sliced okra) thoroughly in blender.

6. Transfer the wet mixture to the bowl of dry ingredients. Mix well and quickly.

7. Scrape the batter onto the prepared baking sheet. Push the mixture to the edges, then level with a spatula. Top with okra slices and bake for about 60 minutes or until dry to the touch.

8. Place upside down on a cooling rack. Remove the pan and paper. Let cool.

9. After cooling, cut into desired pieces or use as a prebaked pizza crust. Store in a sealed container in the refrigerator.

Gratitude Herb Bread

MAKES ONE 12 X 17-INCH BREAD

A light, bean-based bread containing onion and the classic herbs dill, sage, and thyme. Taste and smell of holiday stuffing makes this bread perfect for turkey sandwiches—and chicken works, too! Salads become extra special and scrumptious with croutons made from this grain-free, gluten-free bread! Or use as a lovely toast to accompany breakfast.

DRY INGREDIENTS

1 cup raw, shell-free sunflower seeds

3 cups golden flaxseed meal

½ teaspoon fresh or dried sage

1 teaspoon fresh or dried thyme

2 tablespoons onion powder

1 teaspoon baking soda

2 teaspoons baking powder

1 teaspoon sea salt

WET INGREDIENTS

1¼ cups cooked Great Northern beans, or 1 (15.8-ounce) can, drained and rinsed

1 cup chopped celery

1 cup chopped zucchini

4 large eggs

2 tablespoons vinegar

1. Preheat the oven to 350°F.

2. Cover a 12 x 17-inch baking sheet with Pan Lining Paper, foil side down.

3. Grind sunflower seeds into a fine meal.

4. In a large bowl, mix together the dry ingredients.

5. Blend wet ingredients thoroughly in blender.

6. Transfer the wet mixture to the bowl of dry ingredients. Mix well and quickly.

7. Scrape the batter onto the prepared baking sheet. Push the mixture to the edges, then level with a spatula. Bake for about 45 minutes or until dry to the touch.

8. Place upside down on a cooling rack. Remove the pan and paper. Let cool.

9. After cooling, cut into desired pieces or use as a prebaked pizza crust. Store in a sealed container in the refrigerator.

Asian Kale Bread

MAKES ONE 12 X 17-INCH BREAD

Tasty, nutritious, and filling, kale bread can keep you going all day with steady energy, or just reduces that hungry feeling between meals. Perfect for tuna salad and chicken salad sandwiches. Eat plain, grilled, or toasted with soup. Also makes a delicious alternative prebaked bottom for your special homemade pizzas, such as Mongolian barbecue pizza.

DRY INGREDIENTS

1 cup raw, shell-free pumpkin seeds

1½ cups flaxseed meal

1 teaspoon each, organic lemongrass and ginger teas (about 1 teabag each)

1 teaspoon dehydrated or powdered garlic

2 tablespoons whole sesame seeds (optional)

1 teaspoon baking soda

1½ teaspoons baking powder

1 teaspoon sea salt

WET INGREDIENTS

3 medium eggs

1 cup chopped red bell pepper

1 tablespoon vinegar

11 cups fresh baby kale leaves or chopped curly kale (5–6 ounces)

2 cups chopped fresh stir-fry vegetables (broccoli, carrots, snow peas)

1. Preheat the oven to 350°F.

2. Cover a 12 x 17-inch baking sheet with Pan Lining Paper, foil side down.

3. Grind pumpkin seeds into a fine meal.

4. In a large bowl, mix together the dry ingredients.

5. In a blender, combine wet ingredients in order listed. Blend very well, completely breaking up the fresh vegetables into the liquid.

6. Transfer the vegetable mixture to the bowl of dry ingredients. Mix quickly and well.

7. Scrape the batter onto the prepared baking sheet. Push the mixture to the edges, then level with a spatula. Bake for about 50 minutes or until dry to the touch.

8. Place upside down on a cooling rack. Remove the pan and paper. Let cool.

9. After cooling, cut into desired pieces or use as a prebaked pizza crust. Store in a sealed container in the refrigerator.

Tomato Sauce Bread

MAKES ONE 9 X 13-INCH BREAD

Slightly red in color, this bread makes a perfect partner for classic sandwiches like bacon-lettuce-tomato, toasted cheese, hamburgers and cheeseburgers, chicken and eggplant parmesan, and generally any food that appreciates an enhanced tomato flavor. This bread makes a perfect prebaked pizza crust.

DRY INGREDIENTS

1½ cups golden flaxseed meal

¼ teaspoon baking soda

1 teaspoon baking powder

½ teaspoon sea salt

WET INGREDIENTS

1¼ cups cooked Great Northern beans, or 1 (15.8-ounce) can, drained and rinsed

1 (8-ounce) can tomato sauce

⅓ cup liquid egg whites

1 teaspoon vinegar

1. Preheat the oven to 350°F.

2. Cover a 9 x 13-inch baking sheet with Pan Lining Paper, foil side down.

3. In a medium bowl, mix together the dry ingredients.

4. Blend wet ingredients thoroughly in blender.

5. Transfer the wet mixture to the bowl of dry ingredients. Mix well and quickly.

6. Scrape the batter onto the prepared baking sheet. Push the mixture to the edges, then level with a spatula. Bake for about 60 minutes or until dry to the touch.

7. Place upside down on a cooling rack. Remove the pan and paper. Let cool.

8. After cooling, cut into desired pieces or use as a prebaked pizza crust. Store in a sealed container in the refrigerator.

NOTE: To prepare the acorn squash: Wash the outside skin of the squash clean. Cut in half. Scrape out the seeded areas. Cut the squash into 1-inch slices. Broil at 450°F for 15 minutes on a cookie sheet. Let cool. Remove the hard stems. Place in a large measuring cup. Press firmly and mash to remove all air pockets. Measure 2 cups.

Acorn Squash Bread

MAKES ONE 12 X 17-INCH BREAD

A unique bread made with acorn squash and its skin. Light in color and flavor, this bread makes a great mild bread to accompany soups and salads, and turn into sandwiches. The dark flecks of skin throughout the bread are a nice decorative addition when turning the bread into croutons. Perfect for snacks, sandwiches, toast, and prebaked pizza crust.

DRY INGREDIENTS

1 cup raw, shell-free pumpkin seeds

2 cups golden flaxseed meal

½ teaspoon ground ginger

¼ teaspoon ground nutmeg

1 teaspoon baking soda

1½ teaspoons baking powder

½ teaspoon sea salt

WET INGREDIENTS

2 cups cooked, seeded acorn squash with skin (from 1½ pounds raw, stem-free, seed-free squash; see note)

½ cup liquid egg whites

1 tablespoon vinegar

1. Preheat the oven to 350°F.

2. Cover a 12 x 17-inch baking sheet with Pan Lining Paper, foil side down.

3. Grind pumpkin seeds into a fine meal.

4. In a large bowl, mix together the dry ingredients.

5. Blend wet ingredients thoroughly in blender.

6. Transfer the wet mixture to the bowl of dry ingredients. Mix well and quickly.

7. Scrape the batter onto the prepared baking sheet. Push the mixture to the edges, then level with a spatula. Bake for about 30 minutes or until dry to the touch.

8. Place upside down on a cooling rack. Remove the pan and paper. Let cool.

9. After cooling, cut into desired pieces or use as a prebaked pizza crust. Store in a sealed container in the refrigerator.

Garlic Onion Bread

MAKES ONE 12 X 17-INCH BREAD

Baked garlic and onion makes a mouthwatering bread. A favorite for the whole family!

Perfect for burgers, sandwiches, pizzas, croutons, breadsticks, and more!

It really just goes with practically everything. The aroma will call everyone to dinner;

the taste will keep them at the table, asking for more.

DRY INGREDIENTS

2 cups raw, shell-free sunflower seeds

2 cups golden flaxseed meal

2 tablespoons fresh or dried dill

1 teaspoon baking soda

1 teaspoon baking powder

½ teaspoon sea salt

WET INGREDIENTS

2 cups chopped yellow onion

10 garlic cloves

1 cup liquid egg whites

2 tablespoons vinegar

1. Preheat the oven to 350°F.

2. Cover a 12 x 17-inch baking sheet with Pan Lining Paper, foil side down.

3. Grind sunflower seeds into a fine meal.

4. In a large bowl mix together dry ingredients.

5. Blend wet ingredients thoroughly in blender.

6. Transfer the wet ingredients to the bowl of dry ingredients. Mix quickly and well.

7. Scrape the batter on to the prepared baking sheet. Push the mixture to the edges, then level the thickness with a spatula.

8. Bake for 30 minutes or until dry to the touch.

9. Place upside down on a cooling rack. Remove the pan and paper. Let cool.

10. After cooling, cut into desired pieces or use as a prebaked pizza crust. Store in a sealed container in the refrigerator.

Ranch Onion Bread

MAKES ONE 9 X 13-INCH BREAD

All the ingredients that make the traditional ranch flavor so great! Turns ordinary sandwiches into a special treat. Perfect for grain-free, gluten-free croutons, or as an accompaniment to salads and soups. When used as prebaked pizza crust, homemade pizzas become special and memorable. This bread really delivers with aroma and taste!

DRY INGREDIENTS

½ cup raw, shell-free sunflower seeds

1½ cups flaxseed meal

1½ teaspoons fresh or dried parsley

1½ teaspoons fresh or dried dill

1½ teaspoons garlic powder

½ teaspoon baking soda

½ teaspoon baking powder

½ teaspoon sea salt

WET INGREDIENTS

½ cup chopped onion

½ cup chopped zucchini

½ cup chopped carrot

¼ cup sour cream

¼ cup liquid egg whites

1 tablespoon vinegar

1. Preheat the oven to 350°F.

2. Cover a 9 x 13-inch baking sheet with Pan Lining Paper, foil side down.

3. Grind sunflower seeds into a fine meal.

4. In a medium bowl, mix together the dry ingredients.

5. Blend wet ingredients thoroughly in blender.

6. Transfer the wet mixture to the bowl of dry ingredients. Mix well and quickly.

7. Scrape the batter onto the prepared baking sheet. Push the mixture to the edges, then level with a spatula. Bake for about 45 minutes or until dry to the touch.

8. Place upside down on a cooling rack. Remove the pan and paper. Let cool.

9. After cooling, cut into desired pieces or use as a prebaked pizza crust. Store in a sealed container in the refrigerator.

Lemon Garlic Spinach Bread

MAKES ONE 9 X 13-INCH BREAD

Let this classic combination of flavors lull you into that feeling of 5-star restaurants' serving you a yummy side dish, spinach drizzled with a lemon garlic butter sauce. Eat the bread plain; as toast, sandwiches, or bite-size snacks; or make croutons.

DRY INGREDIENTS

1½ cups flaxseed meal

½ teaspoon baking soda

½ teaspoon baking powder

¼ teaspoon sea salt

WET INGREDIENTS

⅓ cup chopped tomato

5 garlic cloves

11 cups fresh baby spinach (5–6 ounces)

¼ cup liquid egg whites

2 teaspoons lemon zest

1½ teaspoons white vinegar

1. Preheat the oven to 350°F.

2. Cover a 9 x 13-inch baking sheet with Pan Lining Paper, foil side down.

3. In a medium bowl, mix together the dry ingredients.

4. Blend wet ingredients thoroughly in blender.

5. Transfer the wet mixture to the bowl of dry ingredients. Mix well and quickly.

6. Scrape the batter onto the prepared baking sheet. Push the mixture to the edges, then level with a spatula. Bake for about 60 minutes or until dry to the touch.

7. Place upside down on a cooling rack. Remove the pan and paper. Let cool.

8. After cooling, cut into desired pieces or use as a prebaked pizza crust. Store in a sealed container in the refrigerator.

Croutons

Bread-free bread croutons are guilt-free additions to any soup or salad. Made from any
bread-free bread sandwich bread recipe. Just cut the bread
into desired crouton-size cubes and pop into the oven for a few minutes.

DRY INGREDIENTS

**3 cups cubed bread-free
bread (sandwich bread)**

1. Preheat the oven to 300°F.

2. Place the cubes on a 12 x 17-inch baking sheet.

3. Bake thinner breads for 15 minutes, thicker breads
for 30 minutes.

4. Let cool on the baking sheet.

5. After cooling, store in a sealed container in the
refrigerator.

QUICK BREADS & MUFFINS

Fresh Sweet Corn Bread

MAKES ONE 8-INCH SQUARE BREAD

A naturally sweet, bright yellow, corn bread that tastes just like
corn on the cob. Unlike traditional corn bread, this fresh corn bread is gluten free,
sugar free, dairy free, and is bursting with fresh corn flavor.

DRY INGREDIENTS

1½ cups corn flour, or fine yellow cornmeal

1 teaspoon baking powder

1 teaspoon baking soda

½ teaspoon sea salt

WET INGREDIENTS

3 cups fresh sweet corn (from 4 to 5 ears corn; see note)

½ cup liquid egg whites

2 tablespoons vinegar

3 tablespoons your favorite flavored oil, or butter

1. Preheat the oven to 375°F.

2. In a large, heat–resistant, nonreactive bowl, such as ceramic or stainless steel, combine the corn flour, baking soda, baking powder, and salt. Stir thoroughly. Set aside.

3. In a blender, combine the corn, egg whites, and vinegar. Blend well.

4. Heat the oil in oven in an 8-inch square baking pan until hot, 2 to 3 minutes. Remove from the oven and place on a hot pad.

5. Transfer the fresh corn mixture to the bowl of dry ingredients. Mix quickly and well. Next, pour two-thirds of the hot oil from the baking pan into the bowl of batter. Mix well.

6. Now, transfer the batter from the bowl to the baking pan. Distribute evenly.

7. Bake for 20 to 30 minutes, or 15 to 20 minutes if using frozen corn. Test the center with a toothpick; it should come out clean.

8. Serve immediately, or let cool. Store in a sealed container in the refrigerator.

NOTE: If you choose to use frozen sweet corn instead, measure 2 cups of frozen corn first, then thaw it.

Sunflower Zucchini Loaf with Pine Nuts

MAKES ONE 8½ X 4½-INCH LOAF

Definitely not Mom's traditional fare—this quick bread is an upscale treat that's great with soup, or alone as a hearty vegetarian treat. Serve as a side with tuna and chicken salads. You can use as a corn-free, grain-free and gluten-free holiday dressing.

DRY INGREDIENTS

½ cup toasted pine nuts

1 teaspoon fennel seeds

1¾ cups raw, shell-free sunflower seeds

2 tablespoons coconut flour

2 teaspoons baking powder

½ teaspoon baking soda

¼ teaspoon sea salt

WET INGREDIENTS

2 cups coarsely grated zucchini (8 ounces zucchini)

3 large eggs

2 tablespoons fresh lemon juice

¼ cup golden raisins

1. Preheat the oven to 400°F.

2. Place the grated zucchini on a paper towel to absorb excess moisture, then transfer to a small bowl. Set aside.

3. Toast the pine nuts in a small, dry skillet on medium-high heat for 2 to 3 minutes. Slide the pan back and forth to prevent burning. Let cool. Chop into much smaller pieces.

4. Grind the fennel seeds along with sunflower seeds to make a medium-coarse meal, using a food processor.

5. In a large bowl, combine the herbed sunflower seed meal, toasted pine nuts, coconut flour, baking powder, baking soda, and salt. Mix well.

6. In a blender, combine the eggs, lemon juice, and golden raisins. Blend well breaking raisins into small bits.

7. Transfer the egg mixture to the bowl of zucchini. Mix just to coat the zucchini.

8. Grease an 8½ x 4½ loaf pan well, using butter or solid coconut oil.

9. Pour the zucchini mixture into the bowl of dry ingredients. Mix well.

10. Transfer to the prepared loaf pan.

11. Bake for 30 minutes.

12. Store in a sealed container in the refrigerator.

Garlic Buttered Mushroom Loaf

MAKES ONE 8½ X 4½-INCH LOAF

A side bread that conjures up images of wine, steaks, and cozy fireplaces. A dense moist and "meaty" quick bread filled with eight ounces of white mushrooms held together by the flavors of garlic and basil.

DRY INGREDIENTS

2 cups almond meal

½ cup chia seed meal

2 tablespoons garlic powder

1 tablespoon dried basil

1½ teaspoons KAL nutritional yeast or your favorite imitation butter powder

1 teaspoon baking soda

1 teaspoon baking powder

½ teaspoon sea salt

WET INGREDIENTS

8 ounces fresh white button mushrooms

2 large eggs

¼ cup rice or wine vinegar

1. Preheat the oven to 350°F.

2. Grease an 8½ x 4½ loaf pan well, using butter or solid coconut oil.

3. In a large bowl, combine the almond flour, chia seed meal, garlic powder, basil, nutritional yeast, baking soda, baking powder, and salt. Mix well. Set aside.

4. In a blender, combine the mushrooms, eggs, and vinegar. Blend on high speed until foamy.

5. Transfer the mushroom mixture to the bowl of dry ingredients. Mix well.

6. Pour into the prepared loaf pan.

7. Bake for 35 minutes.

8. Serve hot. Store in a sealed container in the refrigerator.

Cranberry, Carrot & Lemon Bread

MAKES ONE 8½ X 4½-INCH LOAF

Wonderful as an appetizer, a snack on the go, or an after-dinner treat.
Serve with ice cream or add your favorite spread. A sweet, moist treat everyone will
love. The outer layer is crispy, adding a nice texture. No grain, no cane, just
naturally sweetened bread. No one will guess it's wheat, gluten, and sugar free.

DRY INGREDIENTS

2½ cups almond meal

2 teaspoons baking powder

¾ teaspoon baking soda

¼ teaspoon sea salt

WET INGREDIENTS

1 cup coarsely grated carrot

3 large eggs

2 tablespoons fresh lemon juice

¼ teaspoon lemon oil

¼ cup club soda

⅓ cup dried cranberries

1. Preheat the oven to 375°F.

2. Place the grated carrot on a paper towel to absorb excess moisture.

3. In a large bowl, combine the carrots, almond meal, baking powder, baking soda, and salt.

4. Grease an 8½ x 4½ loaf pan, using butter or solid coconut oil.

5. In a blender, combine the eggs, lemon juice, lemon oil, club soda, and dried cranberries. Blend well, starting on low speed but progressing to high so the cranberries convert to tiny bits.

6. Transfer to the prepared loaf pan.

7. Bake for 40 minutes.

8. Serve hot or cold. Store in a sealed container in the refrigerator.

Parmesan Pepper Zucchini Bread

MAKES ONE 8½ X 4½-INCH LOAF

The coarse grind of the seeds lends the bread a chewy, nutty texture
with a dense, heavy artisan feel. Filling and satisfying. The perfect accompaniment
for Italian food, fish, and soups.

DRY INGREDIENTS

2½ cups raw, shell-free pumpkin seeds

½ cup grated Parmesan cheese, plus more to taste

1 teaspoon ground black pepper

¾ teaspoon baking soda

2 teaspoons baking powder

¼ cup chia seed meal

WET INGREDIENTS

1½ cups coarsely grated zucchini (6 ounces zucchini)

3 large eggs

2 tablespoons vinegar

2 tablespoons olive oil

1. Preheat the oven to 400°F.

2. Place the grated zucchini on a paper towel to absorb excess moisture, then transfer to a small bowl. Set aside.

3. Grind the pumpkin seeds with a food processor until they are coarsely ground.

4. In a large bowl, combine the pumpkin seed meal, the ½ cup of grated Parmesan, black pepper, baking soda, and baking powder. Mix well.

5. In a blender, combine the eggs, vinegar, olive oil, and chia seed meal and blend until mixed.

6. Grease an 8½ x 4½ loaf pan, using butter or solid coconut oil.

7. Toss the zucchini with the dry ingredients and mix well. Now add the egg mixture. Mix well.

8. Pour the batter into the prepared loaf pan. Sprinkle the top with Parmesan cheese.

9. Bake for 40 minutes.

10. Serve hot or cold. Store in a sealed container in the refrigerator.

Banana Bread

No grain, no cane, banana bread. A delicious treat that you and your kids will love.
No one will guess it's wheat, gluten, and sugar free.

DRY INGREDIENTS

2 cups almond meal

¾ cups flaxseed meal

2 teaspoons ground cinnamon

½ teaspoon pure stevia powder

½ cup chopped pecans

1 teaspoon baking soda

2 teaspoons baking powder

WET INGREDIENTS

1½ cups mashed very ripe banana (see note)

¼ cup liquid egg whites

2 teaspoons vanilla extract

1 tablespoon vinegar

2 tablespoons salted butter or solid coconut oil

1. Preheat the oven to 350°F.

2. In a large bowl, combine the almond meal, flaxseed meal, cinnamon, stevia, chopped pecans, baking soda, and baking powder. Mix well. Set aside.

3. In a blender, combine the banana, liquid egg whites, vanilla, and vinegar. Blend on high speed for about a minute to allow the egg whites and banana to gain some volume with air bubbles.

4. Place the butter in an 8½ x 4½ loaf pan and melt in the oven, 2 to 3 minutes.

5. While the butter is melting, transfer the banana mixture to the bowl of dry ingredients and mix well.

6. Transfer the loaf pan from the oven to a hot pad and empty the batter into the loaf pan. Do not stir.

7. Bake for 45 minutes to 1 hour.

8. Serve hot or cold. Store in a sealed container in the refrigerator.

NOTE: Banana bread is best when made with really ripe (dark-spotted) bananas. To speed up the ripening process, mash regular bananas in a measuring cup until you have 1½ cups. Cover loosely with a cloth and let it sit on your kitchen counter all day. The top will become dark and a hint of alcohol smell will form. After aging to your desired degree, just place in the fridge overnight or for a couple of days, until you are ready to make the bread.

Dark Spicy Banana Bread

MAKES ONE 8½ X 4½-INCH LOAF

For experimental adults who aren't afraid of flavors they will dream about.

DRY INGREDIENTS

2 cups almond meal

1 cup flaxseed meal

2 teaspoons ground cinnamon

1 tablespoon brown sugar (optional)

¼ teaspoon ground nutmeg

½ teaspoon cayenne

⅛ teaspoon pure stevia powder

½ cup chopped pecans

2 teaspoons baking powder

1 teaspoon baking soda

WET INGREDIENTS

1½ cups mashed very ripe banana (see note, opposite page)

¼ cup liquid egg whites

2 teaspoons vanilla extract

1 tablespoon rum extract

1 tablespoon vinegar

2 tablespoons salted butter, or solid coconut oil

1. Preheat the oven to 350°F.

2. In a large bowl, combine the almond meal, flaxseed meal, cinnamon, brown sugar (optional), nutmeg, cayenne, stevia, pecans, baking soda, and baking powder. Mix well. Set aside.

3. In a blender, combine the banana, egg whites, vanilla, rum extract, and vinegar. Blend well on high speed, allowing the egg whites and banana to gain some volume with air bubbles.

4. Place the butter in an 8½ x 4½ loaf pan and melt in the oven, 2 to 3 minutes.

5. While the butter is melting, transfer the banana mixture to the bowl of dry ingredients and mix well.

6. Transfer the loaf pan from the oven to a hot pad and empty the batter into the loaf pan.

7. Bake for 35 minutes.

8. Serve hot or cold. The flavors become more intense after sitting overnight. Store in a sealed container in the refrigerator.

Cinnamon Apple Raisin Bread

MAKES ONE 9 X 13-INCH BREAD

A classic bread packed full of apples, cinnamon, and raisins.

Thin, sturdy, and flavorful. The raisins make it naturally sweet. A great children's treat.

Add peanut butter and make it a meal.

DRY INGREDIENTS

1½ cups golden flaxseed meal

1 teaspoon ground cinnamon

1 teaspoon baking soda

¼ teaspoon sea salt

WET INGREDIENTS

½ cup raisins

1 teaspoon fresh lemon juice

4 cups cored and chopped red apple, not peeled

¼ cup liquid egg whites

1. Preheat the oven to 350°F.

2. Cover a 9 x 13-inch baking sheet with Pan Lining Paper, foil side down. Press the paper into the form of the baking sheet.

3. In a medium bowl, combine the flaxseed meal, raisins, cinnamon, baking soda, and salt. Mix well. Set aside.

4. In a blender, combine the lemon juice, chopped apples, and egg whites. Blend well.

5. Pour the pureed apple into the bowl of dry ingredients. Mix quickly.

6. Transfer the batter to the prepared baking sheet. Push the mixture to the edges, then use a spatula to level the thickness.

7. Bake for 50–60 minutes.

8. Place upside down on a cooling rack. Remove the pan and paper. Let cool.

9. The bread becomes more flavorful after it has cooled. Cut into desired pieces. Store in a sealed container in the refrigerator.

Lemon Strawberry Bread

MAKES ONE 9 X 13-INCH BREAD

This delicious fruit bread is a children's favorite as it mimics the sweetness
of store-bought breads. Perfect as a sweet hamburger bun, sweet toast, with butter
or cheese spreads, and more!

DRY INGREDIENTS

1½ cups golden flaxseed meal

1 teaspoon baking powder

1 teaspoon baking soda

¼ teaspoon sea salt

1 teaspoon cane sugar (optional)

WET INGREDIENTS

½ cup liquid egg whites

1 ¾ cups coarsely chopped fresh strawberries

¼ teaspoon vanilla extract

2 teaspoons lemon zest

1 teaspoon fresh lemon juice

1. Preheat the oven to 400°F.

2. Cover a 9 x 13-inch baking sheet with Pan Lining Paper, foil side down. Press the paper into the form of the baking sheet.

3. In a medium bowl, combine the flaxseed meal, baking powder, baking soda, and salt. Mix well. Set aside.

4. In a blender, combine the egg whites, cane sugar (optional), strawberries, vanilla, lemon zest, and lemon juice. Blend well.

5. Pour the strawberry mixture into the bowl of dry ingredients. Mix quickly.

6. Transfer the batter to the prepared baking sheet. Push the mixture to the edges, then use a spatula to level the thickness.

7. Bake for 30 minutes.

8. Place upside down on a cooling rack. Remove the pan and paper. Let cool.

9. The bread tastes best after it has cooled. Cut into desired pieces. Store in a sealed container in the refrigerator.

Orange Spice Bread

MAKES ONE 9 X 13-INCH BREAD

A sweet, delightful aroma and a slightly sticky texture conjure up images of desserts.
This bread makes a great partner for cheese spreads, jellies, and jams, but also, it will
add a new level to your French toast (as shown, opposite).

DRY INGREDIENTS

1½ cups golden flaxseed meal

1 teaspoon ground cinnamon

¼ teaspoon ground nutmeg

¼ teaspoon ground cloves

1 teaspoon baking powder

1 teaspoon baking soda

¼ teaspoon sea salt

1 tablespoon brown sugar (optional)

WET INGREDIENTS

½ cup liquid egg whites

1½ cups peeled, seeded, and coarsely chopped orange

¼ teaspoon vanilla extract

2 teaspoons orange extract, or orange zest

1 teaspoon fresh lemon juice

1. Preheat the oven to 400°F.

2. Cover a 9 x 13-inch baking sheet with Pan Lining Paper, foil side down. Press the paper into the form of the baking sheet.

3. In a medium bowl, combine the flaxseed meal, cinnamon, nutmeg, cloves, baking powder, baking soda, and salt. Mix well. Set aside.

4. In a blender, combine the egg whites, brown sugar (optional), chopped orange, vanilla, orange extract, and lemon juice. Blend well.

5. Pour the orange mixture into the bowl of dry ingredients. Mix quickly.

6. Transfer the batter to the prepared baking sheet. Push the mixture to the edges, then use a spatula to level the thickness.

7. Bake for 30 minutes.

8. Place upside down on a cooling rack. Remove the pan and paper. Let cool.

9. The bread tastes best after it has cooled. Cut into desired pieces. Store in a sealed container in the refrigerator.

10. For French Toast, follow your favorite recipe, using this bread in place of traditional bread.

Spicy Sweet Corn Muffins

MAKES 12 MUFFINS

Delicate and full of fresh corn flavor. These muffins are perfect plain
or with honey butter at every meal.

DRY INGREDIENTS

1½ cups corn flour

1 teaspoon guar gum

1 teaspoon baking powder

1½ teaspoons sea salt

WET INGREDIENTS

1 cup diced red bell pepper

1 tablespoon seeded and minced jalapeño pepper

3 cups fresh sweet corn (from 4 to 5 ears corn)

4 large eggs

1. Preheat the oven to 425°F.

2. In a medium bowl, combine the corn flour, red bell pepper, jalapeño, guar gum, baking powder, and salt. Mix well. Set aside.

3. In a blender, combine fresh corn, and eggs. Blend well.

4. Transfer the corn mixture to the pepper mixture and mix well.

5. Spoon into a greased 12-cup muffin tin, filling each cup three-quarters full.

6. Bake for 15 minutes.

7. Serve warm, or let cool. Store in a sealed container in the refrigerator.

Blueberry Lemon Muffins

MAKES 12 MUFFINS

Gentle lemon flavor caresses the plentiful and sweet bursting blueberries in every bite.

These delicate light muffins hold together well—no crumbs.

Grain free and sugar free and satisfying.

DRY INGREDIENTS

3 cups almond meal

1 tablespoon baking powder

WET INGREDIENTS

1½ cups liquid egg whites

2 tablespoons vanilla extract

1 tablespoon lemon zest

1½ cups fresh blueberries

1. Preheat the oven to 350°F.

2. In a medium bowl, combine the almond meal and baking powder. Mix well. Set aside.

3. In a blender, combine the egg whites, vanilla, and lemon zest. Blend well, creating a foamy liquid.

4. Transfer the egg white mixture to the bowl of dry ingredients. Mix well. Stir in the blueberries.

5. Spoon into a greased 12-cup muffin tin, filling each cup full. Heaping full is also okay.

6. Bake for 20 minutes.

7. Serve warm, or let cool. Store in a sealed container in the refrigerator.

Soy Nut Okra Muffins

MAKES 12 MUFFINS

A hearty taste of roasted soy nuts combines with a moist muffin for breakfast, lunch, dinner, and a healthy snack. Even people who don't like okra love this muffin because they don't taste the okra! A mild flavor and a big texture make these a hearty versatile brown bag addition.

DRY INGREDIENTS

1¾ cups whole roasted salted soy nuts

2 teaspoons baking powder

2 teaspoons guar gum

½ teaspoon onion powder

½ teaspoon sea salt

WET INGREDIENTS

1½ cups chopped fresh okra (about 4 ounces)

¼ cup chopped red bell pepper

1 cup liquid egg whites

2 tablespoons sunflower oil

1. Preheat the oven to 350°F.

2. Place cupcake liners in 12-cup muffin tin.

3. Grind the soy nuts into a fine meal.

4. Combine the soy nut meal, baking powder, guar gum, onion powder, and salt in a large bowl. Mix well.

5. In a blender, combine the okra, bell pepper, egg whites, and sunflower oil. The mixture will be very thick and sticky.

6. Add the okra mixture to the dry ingredients. Fold the wet and dry ingredients together until well mixed.

7. Scoop the batter to fill one cupcake liner, clipping the mixture off with the edge of a spoon. Do same with the remaining liners.

8. Bake for 30 minutes.

9. Serve warm, or let cool. Store in a sealed container in the refrigerator.

CRACKERS & BISCUITS

Garlic Pumpkin Seed Crackers

MAKES 35 TO 45 (2-INCH) CRACKERS

Crunchy grain-free crackers. Simple ingredients and topped with garlic.
A favorite at home and at parties.

DRY INGREDIENTS

1 cup raw, shell-free pumpkin seeds

¼ teaspoon sea salt

2 tablespoons dehydrated garlic pieces

WET INGREDIENTS

3 tablespoons water

1. Preheat the oven to 300°F.

2. Grind pumpkin seeds into a fine meal.

3. In a small bowl, combine the pumpkin seed meal, water, and salt. Mix well until the mixture comes together into a ball.

4. Tear two sheets of Pan Lining Paper big enough to cover a 12 x 17-inch cookie sheet.

5. Place the dough between the two sheets with the parchment sides touching the dough. Push the dough flat with your hands, then use a rolling pin until the dough is about ⅛ inch thick.

6. Peel away the top paper gently. Some outer edges of the rolled dough may look thinner. Use a rubber spatula to push all the thin edges toward the center of the dough. Smooth the edges with the spatula, or reapply the top paper and gently press the edges with your hands. This step helps prevent the outer crackers from having burnt edges. Optional: Lightly score the dough into squares. Press firmly and quickly with a pizza cutter for straight edges, or use a pasta roller for jagged edges.

7. Sprinkle the dehydrated garlic pieces across the top. Place the top sheet of paper back on top, and press gently, then remove the top paper.

8. Slide the bottom paper, with its dough, onto a 12 x 17-inch cookie sheet.

9. Bake for 15 minutes.

10. Let cool for 30 minutes, then break into pieces by hand. Store in a sealed container.

Pumpkin Seed Crackers

MAKES 35 TO 45 (2-INCH) CRACKERS

A most simple cracker—pumpkin seeds, water, and salt. Quick, easy, and very tasty!

DRY INGREDIENTS

1 cup raw, shell-free pumpkin seeds

¼ teaspoon sea salt

WET INGREDIENTS

3 tablespoons water

1. Preheat the oven to 300°F.

2. Grind the pumpkin seeds into a fine meal.

3. In a small bowl, combine the pumpkin seed meal, water, and salt. Mix well until the mixture comes together into a ball.

4. Tear two sheets of Pan Lining Paper big enough to cover a 12 x 17-inch cookie sheet.

5. Place the dough between the two sheets with the parchment sides touching the dough. Push the dough flat with your hands, then use a rolling pin until the dough is about ⅛ inch thick.

6. Peel away the top paper gently. Some outer edges of the rolled dough may look thinner. Use a rubber spatula to push all the thin edges toward the center of the dough. Smooth the edges with the spatula, or reapply the top paper and gently press the edges with your hands. This step helps prevent the outer crackers from having burnt edges. Optional: Lightly score the dough into squares. Press firmly and quickly with a pizza cutter for straight edges, or use a pasta roller for jagged edges.

7. Slide the bottom paper, with its dough, onto a 12 x 17-inch cookie sheet.

8. Bake for 15 minutes.

9. Let cool for 30 minutes, then break into pieces by hand. Store in a sealed container.

Zesty Cranberry Pumpkin Seed Crackers

MAKES 35 TO 45 (2-INCH) CRACKERS

Pumpkin and cranberry make a magnificent coupling of flavors, and the
green with red color is perfect for holiday gatherings. A slightly sweet cracker.

DRY INGREDIENTS

**1 cup raw, shell-free
pumpkin seeds**

¼ cup dried cranberries

½ teaspoon sea salt

WET INGREDIENTS

3 tablespoons water

**1 teaspoon packed orange
or lemon zest**

1. Preheat the oven to 300°F.

2. Grind the pumpkin seeds into a fine meal.

3. Chop the dried cranberries into smaller pieces.

4. In a small bowl, combine the pumpkin seed meal, cranberries, orange zest, water, and salt. Mix well until the mixture comes together into a ball.

5. Tear two sheets of Pan Lining Paper big enough to cover a 12 x 17-inch cookie sheet.

6. Place the dough in between the two sheets with the parchment sides touching the dough. Push the dough flat with your hands, then use a rolling pin until the dough is about ⅛ inch thick.

7. Peel away the top paper gently. Some outer edges of the rolled dough may look thinner. Use a rubber spatula to push all the thin edges toward the center of the dough. Smooth the edges with the spatula or reapply the top paper and gently press edges with your hands. This step helps prevent the outer crackers from having burnt edges. Optional: Lightly score the dough into squares. Press firmly and quickly with a pizza cutter for straight edges, or use a pasta roller for jagged edges.

8. Slide the bottom paper, with its dough, onto a 12 x 17-inch cookie sheet.

9. Bake for 15 minutes.

10. Let cool for 30 minutes, then break into pieces by hand. Store in a sealed container.

Roasted Sunflower Seed Crackers

MAKES 35 TO 45 (2-INCH) CRACKERS

This cracker has the same crunch and feel of flour crackers but without any grain or gluten. They are slightly sweetened with sugar, which is used as a binder.

DRY INGREDIENTS

1 cup roasted, salted, shell-free sunflower seeds (see note)

2 tablespoons cane sugar

WET INGREDIENTS

2 tablespoons water

NOTE: Do not use dry-roasted sunflower seeds in this recipe.

1. Preheat the oven to 300°F.

2. Grind sunflower seeds into a fine meal.

3. In a small bowl, combine the sunflower seed meal, water, and cane sugar. Mix well until the mixture comes together into a ball.

4. Tear two sheets of Pan Lining Paper big enough to cover a 12 x 17-inch cookie sheet.

5. Place the dough between the two sheets with the parchment sides touching the dough. Push the dough flat with your hands, then use a rolling pin until the dough is about ⅛ inch thick.

6. Peel away the top paper gently. Some outer edges of the rolled dough may look thinner. Use a rubber spatula to push all the thin edges toward the center of the dough. Smooth the edges with the spatula, or reapply the top paper and gently press the edges with your hands. This step helps prevent the outer crackers from having burnt edges. Optional: Lightly score the dough into squares. Press firmly and quickly with a pizza cutter for straight edges, or use a pasta roller for jagged edges.

7. Slide the bottom paper, with its dough, onto a 12 x 17-inch cookie sheet.

8. Bake for 15 minutes.

9. Let cool for 30 minutes, then break into pieces by hand. Store in a sealed container.

Acorn Squash Biscuits

MAKES 12 BISCUITS

Filling and satisfying. These biscuits are soft and delicious.
Your family will come running for the buttery aroma and flavor, and they
will be satisfied with a soft, fluffy center just like real biscuits.
Eat them plain, add butter or honey, or make biscuit sandwiches.

DRY INGREDIENTS

1 cup raw, shell-free pumpkin seeds

2½ cups golden flaxseed meal

1 teaspoon baking soda

1 tablespoon baking powder

2 tablespoons KAL nutritional yeast, or your favorite imitation powdered butter

½ teaspoon sea salt

WET INGREDIENTS

1¾ cups cooked acorn squash (from 18 ounces fresh squash; see note on p. 48)

½ cup liquid egg whites

1 tablespoon vinegar

1. Preheat the oven to 425°F.

2. Grind pumpkin seeds into a fine meal.

3. Cover a 12 x 17-inch baking sheet with parchment.

4. Grease, then lightly flour the inside of a ¼-cup measuring cup. Use your favorite gluten-free flour.

5. In a large bowl, stir together the pumpkin seed meal, flaxseed meal, baking soda, baking powder, nutritional yeast, and salt. Mix well. Set aside.

6. In a blender, combine the squash, egg whites, and vinegar. Blend well.

7. Transfer the squash mixture to the bowl of dry ingredients. Mix quickly and well.

8. Scoop a little dough into the greased and floured measuring cup. This step is to shape the biscuits. Tap once to shape it within cup, then tap again to release the contents to the lined baking sheet. Flour the measuring cup again. Repeat, spacing the biscuits about an inch apart.

9. Bake for 10 to 15 minutes.

10. Serve warm, or let cool. Store in a sealed container in the refrigerator.

Eggplant Biscuits

MAKES 12 BISCUITS

What a delightful way to eat eggplant! The golden color is luring. The texture is the same as that of a biscuit and the delightful flavor hinted with curry keeps them coming back for more. A special dinner treat, perfect for soaking up meat juices.

DRY INGREDIENTS

½ cup coconut flour

1 teaspoon guar gum

1 teaspoon curry powder

2 teaspoons baking powder

½ teaspoon sea salt

WET INGREDIENTS

4 cups peeled, chopped fresh eggplant (10 ounces eggplant)

¼ cup ground raw coconut

8 large eggs

1. Preheat the oven to 425°F.

2. In a blender, combine eggplant, ground raw coconut, and eggs. Blend well. Transfer the mixture to a large bowl.

3. Add to the bowl the coconut flour, guar gum, curry powder, baking powder, and salt. Mix well.

4. Spoon into a greased 12-cup muffin tin, filling each cup three-quarters full. Or just spoon drop the dough onto a 12 x 17-inch cookie sheet lined with parchment paper.

5. Bake for 20 minutes.

6. Serve warm. Store in a sealed container in the refrigerator.

Mushroom Biscuits

MAKES 12 BISCUITS

Simple and delicious. These dark, moist, and fluffy biscuits made with minimal spices
are packed with mushroom flavor and serve as perfect complement for
heavy savory dinners. A delicious match for gravy and fillets served with butter-sautéed
vegetables, or any plate that begs for a wipe-down.

DRY INGREDIENTS

¾ cup coconut flour

2 teaspoons baking powder

WET INGREDIENTS

6 cups washed, chopped or sliced fresh white button mushrooms (1 [16-ounce] container)

8 large eggs

1. Preheat the oven to 425°F.

2. In a blender, combine the mushrooms and eggs. Blend well.

3. Transfer to a large bowl, then add the coconut flour and baking powder. Mix well.

4. Spoon into a greased 12-cup muffin tin, filling each cup almost completely. Or just spoon drop the dough onto a 12 x 17-inch cookie sheet lined with parchment paper.

5. Bake for 20 minutes.

6. Serve warm. Store in a sealed container in the refrigerator.

Cajun Kale Biscuits

MAKES 12 BISCUITS

A visual surprise is only half of this special dinner treat's appeal. Flavored with blackened Cajun spices that are gentle, not harsh, these biscuits work well with other spicy dishes, whether fish, steak, or steamed vegetables.

DRY INGREDIENTS

½ cup coconut flour

½ teaspoon cayenne pepper

2 teaspoons garlic powder

2 teaspoons onion powder

½ teaspoon dried thyme

½ teaspoon dried oregano

½ teaspoon dried basil

½ teaspoon ground black pepper

1 teaspoon guar gum

1 teaspoon baking powder

WET INGREDIENTS

½ cup ground raw coconut

22 cups fresh baby kale leaves or chopped curly kale (10–12 ounces)

8 large eggs

1. Preheat the oven to 425°F.

2. In a large bowl, combine the coconut flour, cayenne, garlic powder, onion powder, thyme, oregano, basil, black pepper, guar gum, and baking powder. Mix well. Set aside.

3. In a blender, combine the raw coconut, kale, and eggs. Blend well.

4. Add the kale mixture to the bowl of dry ingredients and mix well.

5. Spoon into a greased 12-cup muffin tin, filling the cups half-full, or spoon drop on a 12 x 17-inch cookie sheet lined with parchment paper.

6. Bake for 15 minutes.

7. Serve warm, or let cool. Store in a sealed container in the refrigerator.

White Bean Biscuits

These classic biscuits are moist and fluffy. Made to be plain in look and flavor
just like traditional biscuits.

DRY INGREDIENTS

¼ cup coconut flour

2 teaspoons baking powder

1 teaspoon guar gum

WET INGREDIENTS

2 tablespoons ground raw coconut

4 eggs

2 cups cooked Great Northern beans, drained and rinsed

1. Preheat the oven to 425°F.

2. In a blender, combine the beans, raw coconut, and eggs. Blend well.

3. Transfer to a medium bowl and add the coconut flour, baking powder, and guar gum. Mix well.

4. Spoon into a greased 12-cup muffin tin, filling each cup half-full, or spoon drop onto a 12 x 17-inch cookie sheet lined with parchment paper.

5. Bake for 20 minutes.

6. Serve warm, or let cool. Store in a sealed container in the refrigerator.

Sausage Cheddar Biscuits

MAKES 12 BISCUITS

A wonderful breakfast, meal on the run, or meal addition.
You would never guess it was made with beans and raw coconut. Tastes great fresh
from the oven or pulled from a lunch bag.

DRY INGREDIENTS

½ cup coconut flour

1 tablespoon baking powder

1½ teaspoon guar gum

WET INGREDIENTS

¾ cup shredded Cheddar cheese

1½ cups finely diced cooked sausage

¾ cup cooked Great Northern beans, drained and rinsed

2½ cups liquid egg whites

6 tablespoons ground raw coconut

3 pitted dried dates, chopped small

1. Preheat the oven to 425°F.

2. In a medium bowl, stir together the coconut flour, baking powder, guar gum, cheese, and sausage pieces. Mix well. Set aside.

3. In a blender, combine the beans, egg whites, raw coconut, and date pieces. Blend very well.

4. Add the bean mixture to the sausage mixture. Mix well.

5. Spoon into a greased 12-cup muffin tin, filling each cup full.

6. Bake for 15 minutes.

7. Serve warm. Store in a sealed container in the refrigerator.

Cynthia's Single Serving Savory

SERVES 1

A savory take on the mug cake, this little bun has a bite of onion, garlic, and heat from chipotle powder. A perfect side with soups and red meat entrées, or cut in two to hold sausage or beef patties for sliders. Very moist and flexible.

DRY INGREDIENTS

¾ cup Almond Meal (see note)

1 teaspoon baking powder

¼ teaspoon chipotle powder

WET INGREDIENTS

⅓ cup liquid egg whites

⅓ cup diced onion

3 cloves garlic

1 beef bouillon cube

¼ cup shredded Cheddar cheese

1. Combine in a 20-ounce microwave-proof mug or bowl, the almond meal, baking powder, chipotle powder, and ½ of the cheese. Mix well.

2. Combine the egg whites, onion, garlic, and bouillon cube in a single serve blender or immersion stick blender with mixing cup. Blend well.

3. Transfer the onion mixture to the mug of dry ingredients and mix well.

4. Microwave on high for 3 minutes.

5. When the cooking process is complete, remove from the oven and immediately place the remaining cheese on top.

6. Let sit for 5 minutes.

7. Serve warm in mug, or remove. Store in the refrigerator.

NOTE: To make recipe nut-free, grind ¾ cup raw shell-free sunflower seeds into a fine meal to replace almond meal.

TORTILLAS

Introduction to Tortillas

Your tortillas will bake evenly if their thickness is level from edge to edge: the middle not too fat and the edges not too thin. Easier said than done.

Also, note that my recipe yields are for 6-inch tortillas. If you want to make larger tortillas, increase the ingredient amounts proportionally.

HOW TO FORM BREAD-FREE BREAD TORTILLAS

Tear off enough Pan Lining Paper to cover a 12 x 17-inch cookie sheet. Next, tear off a short strip to make a 7 x 15-inch strip. Then cut that strip in two, creating two fat rectangles.

Scoop the "dough" with an ice-cream scoop until you've made the number of scoops specified in the recipe instructions. Or cut into pieces equal in volume, based on your recipe. Place the scooped or cut pieces equal distance apart on the Pan Lining Paper, parchment side up. Take one of your fat rectangles and with its foil side down, facing the dough, press down on the first dough ball.

Now your job is to form the largest tortilla possible without the dough flowing outside the paper. Use your hands, or a rolling pin, or combination as I do. After the dough is shaped, slowly peel away the top paper. Repeat.

After all the tortillas are formed, use a rubber spatula to gently push in any edges that are thinner than the body. The edges need to stay plump to prevent overbaking.

After a few attempts at forming a tortilla by hand or rolling pin, you will pick up a few tricks. One trick is that the edges can be built up while you are molding the tortillas under the paper. Just press and drag the edges back toward the center with your fingers.

Feel free to use a tortilla press. If you do, make sure to cut squares of Pan Lining Paper to form a barrier between the dough and the plates of the press. To make tortillas level when using a press, flip the tortillas after the first pressing, then gently press again. This is because the first press creates a tortilla thicker on one side than on the other, so flipping and making a second, gentle press levels the thickness out.

Black Bean Tortillas

MAKES 10 (6-INCH) TORTILLAS

The healthy international black bean is central to this tortilla.

It's simple ingredients promote versatility. Breakfast tacos, TexMex burritos,

Thai wraps, crunchy tacos & salad bowls, enchiladas . . .

WET INGREDIENTS

1½ cups cooked black beans, or 1 (15-ounce) can, drained and rinsed

½ cup water

½ teaspoon sea salt

DRY INGREDIENTS

½ cup chia seed meal

2½ teaspoons unflavored gelatin

1. In a blender, blend the beans, water, and salt thoroughly, breaking down all bean skin.

2. Transfer to a medium bowl. Whisk in the chia seed meal until the mixture becomes doughlike.

3. Place in a container with a lid and refrigerate for 4 hours, or overnight.

4. Place the chilled dough in a large bowl and fold in the gelatin with your preferred utensil. I use a fork.

5. Preheat the oven to 325°F.

6. Form half of the dough into five tortillas. (See Introduction to Tortillas, page 105.)

7. Place the Pan Lining Paper containing the five tortillas on a 12 x 17-inch cookie sheet.

8. Bake for 12 to 15 minutes.

9. Place the cookie sheet on a hot pad while you turn each tortilla over by carefully lifting it from the parchment before turning it over and placing it back down.

10. Bake for another 5 minutes. Remove from the oven and place the tortillas on a cooling rack.

11. Bake and cool the remaining five tortillas as above.

12. Store in a sealed container in the refrigerator.

Blueberry Tortillas

MAKES 10 (6-INCH) TORTILLAS

Dark blue tortillas that are naturally sweet and hold their contents very well.
Works with most anything you desire, sweet and savory—if you dare.

WET INGREDIENTS

2 cups fresh chilled blueberries

DRY INGREDIENTS

1 cup chia seed meal

2½ teaspoons unflavored gelatin

1. In a blender, blend the blueberries thoroughly.

2. Transfer to a large bowl. Whisk in the chia seed meal until the mixture becomes doughlike.

3. Place in a container with a lid and refrigerate for 4 hours, or overnight.

4. Place the chilled dough in a large bowl and fold in the gelatin with your preferred utensil. I use a fork.

5. Preheat the oven to 325°F.

6. Form half of the dough into five tortillas. (See Introduction to Tortillas, page 105.)

7. Place the Pan Lining Paper containing the five tortillas on a 12 x 17-inch cookie sheet.

8. Bake for 12 to 15 minutes. While baking, form the remaining four tortillas.

9. Place the cookie sheet on a hot pad while you turn each tortilla over by carefully lifting it from the parchment before turning it over and placing it back down.

10. Bake another 5 minutes. Remove from the oven and place the tortillas on a cooling rack.

11. Bake and cool the remaining five tortillas as above.

12. Store in a sealed container in the refrigerator.

Superfood Tortillas

MAKES 6 (6-INCH) TORTILLAS

Super-power your tortilla with superfoods! Make açai, goji, wheat grass, pomegranate, or hemp powder tortillas. A fun way to get your daily dose of superfoods.

WET INGREDIENTS

½ cup water

DRY INGREDIENTS

6 tablespoons superfood powder

1 cup chia seed meal

1½ teaspoons unflavored gelatin

1. In a medium bowl, whisk well the superpowder with the water.

2. Next, add the chia seed meal. Whisk until the mixture becomes doughlike.

3. Place in a container with a lid and refrigerate for 4 hours, or overnight.

4. Place the chilled dough in a large bowl and fold in the gelatin with your preferred utensil. I use a fork.

5. Preheat the oven to 325°F.

6. Form the dough into six tortillas. (See Introduction to Tortillas, page 105.)

7. Place the Pan Lining Paper containing the six tortillas on a 12 x 17-inch cookie sheet.

8. Bake for 12 to 15 minutes.

9. Remove from the oven and place the tortillas on a cooling rack.

10. Store in a sealed container in the refrigerator.

Tomato Sauce Tortillas

MAKES 8 (6-INCH) TORTILLAS

The perfect partner for Tex-Mex foods and any sandwich wrap that could use an extra
tomato flavor boost—this is it!

WET INGREDIENTS

1 cup tomato sauce
(1 [8-ounce] can)

DRY INGREDIENTS

1 cup chia seed meal

2 teaspoons unflavored
gelatin

1. In a medium bowl, combine the tomato sauce and chia seed meal. Whisk until the mixture becomes doughlike.

2. Place in a container with a lid and refrigerate for 4 hours, or overnight.

3. Place the chilled dough in a large bowl and fold in the gelatin with your preferred utensil. I use a fork.

4. Preheat the oven to 325°F.

5. Form half of the dough into four tortillas. (See Introduction to Tortillas, page 105.)

6. Place the Pan Lining Paper containing the four tortillas on a 12 x 17-inch cookie sheet.

7. Bake for 12 to 15 minutes.

8. Place the cookie sheet on a hot pad while you turn each tortilla over by carefully lifting it from the parchment before turning it over and placing it back down.

9. Bake for another 5 minutes. Remove from the oven and place the tortillas on a cooling rack.

10. Bake and cool the remaining tortillas as above.

11. Sotre in a sealed container in the refrigerator.

Cinnamon Banana Tortillas

MAKES 6 (6-INCH) TORTILLAS

A delightful new dessert on the menu! Cinnamon and banana conjure images of apple pie fillings, vanilla ice cream, and spiced whipped cream.

WET INGREDIENTS

¾ cup mashed banana

DRY INGREDIENTS

¾ teaspoon ground cinnamon

½ teaspoon powdered imitation butter

½ cup chia seed meal

1½ teaspoons unflavored gelatin

1. In a medium bowl, combine the banana, cinnamon, imitation butter powder, and chia seed meal. Whisk until the mixture becomes doughlike.

2. Place in a container with a lid and refrigerate for 4 hours, or overnight.

3. Place the chilled dough in a large bowl and fold in the gelatin with your preferred utensil. I use a fork.

4. Preheat the oven to 325°F.

5. Form the dough into six tortillas. (See Introduction to Tortillas, page 105.)

6. Place the Pan Lining Paper containing the six tortillas on a 12 x 17-inch cookie sheet.

7. Bake for 12 to 15 minutes.

8. Place the cookie sheet on a hot pad while you turn each tortilla over by carefully lifting it from the parchment before turning it over and placing it back down.

9. Bake for another 5 minutes. Remove from the oven and place the tortillas on a cooling rack.

10. Store in a sealed container in the refrigerator.

Banana Cranberry Tortillas

MAKES 10 (6-INCH) TORTILLAS

A new holiday favorite! Sweet and colorful. Works with sweet and savory fillings.

WET INGREDIENTS

1 cup fresh whole cranberries

¾ cup mashed ripe banana

1 tablespoon vanilla extract

DRY INGREDIENTS

¾ cup chia seed meal

2½ teaspoons unflavored gelatin

1. In a blender, blend the cranberries, banana, and vanilla thoroughly.

2. Transfer to a medium bowl. Whisk in the chia seed meal until the mixture becomes doughlike.

3. Place in a container with a lid and refrigerate for 4 hours, or overnight.

4. Place the chilled dough in a large bowl and fold in the gelatin with your preferred utensil. I use a fork.

5. Preheat the oven to 325°F.

6. Form half of the dough into five tortillas. (See Introduction to Tortillas, page 105)

7. Place the Pan Lining Paper containing the five tortillas on a 12 x 17-inch cookie sheet.

8. Bake for 12 to 15 minutes. While baking, form the remaining four tortillas.

9. Place the cookie sheet on a hot pad while you turn each tortilla over by carefully lifting it from the parchment before turning it over and placing it back down.

10. Bake for another 5 minutes. Remove from the oven and place the tortillas on a cooling rack.

11. Bake and cool the remaining tortillas as above.

12. Store in a sealed container in the refrigerator.

Fresh Corn Tortillas

MAKES 10 (6-INCH) TORTILLAS

Corn flour is more convenient, but fresh tastes better!

WET INGREDIENTS

2 cups fresh corn (from 3 ears corn)

¼ cup water

DRY INGREDIENTS

1 cup chia seed meal

2½ teaspoons unflavored gelatin

1. In a blender, blend the corn and water thoroughly.

2. Transfer to a medium bowl. Whisk in the chia seed meal until the mixture becomes doughlike.

3. Place in a container with a lid and refrigerate for 4 hours, or overnight.

4. Place the chilled dough in a large bowl and fold in the gelatin with your preferred utensil. I use a fork.

5. Preheat the oven to 325°F.

6. Form half of the dough into five tortillas. (See Introduction to Tortillas, page 105.)

7. Place the Pan Lining Paper containing the five tortillas on a 12 x 17-inch cookie sheet.

8. Bake for 12 to 15 minutes. While baking, form the remaining tortillas.

9. Place the cookie sheet on a hot pad while you turn each tortilla over by carefully lifting it from the parchment before turning it over and placing it back down.

10. Bake for another 5 minutes. Remove from the oven and place the tortillas on a cooling rack.

11. Bake and cool the remaining tortillas as above.

12. Store in a sealed container in the refrigerator.

Garlic Spinach Tortillas

MAKES 8 (6-INCH) TORTILLAS

A delicate colorful green tortilla that doesn't disappoint.

WET INGREDIENTS

11 cups fresh baby spinach leaves (5–6 ounces)

7 garlic cloves

⅓ cup water

DRY INGREDIENTS

¾ cup chia seed meal

¼ teaspoon sea salt

2 teaspoons unflavored gelatin

1. In a blender, blend the spinach, garlic, and water thoroughly.

2. Transfer to a medium bowl. Whisk in the chia seed meal and salt until the mixture becomes doughlike.

3. Place in a container with a lid and refrigerate for 4 hours, or overnight.

4. Place the chilled dough in a large bowl and fold in the gelatin with your preferred utensil. I use a fork.

5. Preheat the oven to 325°F.

6. Form half of the dough into four tortillas. (See Introduction to Tortillas, page 105.)

7. Place the Pan Lining Paper containing the four tortillas on a 12 x 17-inch cookie sheet.

8. Bake for 12–15 minutes. While baking, form the remaining tortillas.

9. Place the cookie sheet on a hot pad while you turn each tortilla over by carefully lifting it from the parchment before turning it over and placing it back down.

10. Bake for another 5 minutes. Remove from the oven and place the tortillas on a cooling rack.

11. Bake and cool the remaining tortillas as above.

12. Store in a sealed container in the refrigerator.

Kale Tortillas

A classic and popular nutritious food that is sure to delight and satisfy.

WET INGREDIENTS

11 cups fresh baby kale leaves or chopped curly kale (5-6 ounces)

½ cup water

DRY INGREDIENTS

1 cup chia seed meal

2 teaspoons unflavored gelatin

1. In a blender, blend the kale and water thoroughly.

2. Transfer to a medium bowl. Whisk in the chia seed meal until the mixture becomes doughlike.

3. Place in a container with a lid and refrigerate for 4 hours, or overnight.

4. Remove from the refrigerator. Place the chilled dough in a large bowl and fold in the gelatin with your preferred utensil. I use a fork.

5. Preheat the oven to 325°F.

6. Form the dough into four tortillas. (See Introduction to Tortillas, page 105.)

7. Place the Pan Lining Paper containing the four tortillas on a 12 x 17-inch cookie sheet.

8. Bake for 12 to 15 minutes.

9. Place the cookie sheet on a hot pad while you turn each tortilla over by carefully lifting it from the parchment before turning it over and placing it back down.

10. Bake for another 5 minutes. Remove from the oven and place the tortillas on a cooling rack.

11. Bake and cool the remaining tortillas as above.

12. Store in a sealed container in the refrigerator.

Mild Pinto Bean Tortillas

MAKES 10 (6-INCH) TORTILLAS

Everything the black bean can do, the pinto can do better!

WET INGREDIENTS

1½ cups cooked pinto beans, or 1 (15-ounce) can, drained and rinsed

2 tablespoons pickled jalapeño slices

½ cup water

DRY INGREDIENTS

½ teaspoon sea salt

¾ cup chia seed meal

2½ teaspoons unflavored gelatin

1. In a blender, blend the beans, pickled jalapeños, water, and salt thoroughly.

2. Transfer to a medium bowl. Whisk in the chia seed meal until the mixture becomes doughlike.

3. Place in a container with a lid and refrigerate for 4 hours, or overnight.

4. Place the chilled dough in a large bowl and fold in the gelatin with your preferred utensil. I use a fork.

5. Preheat the oven to 325°F.

6. Form half of the dough into five tortillas. (See Introduction to Tortillas, page 105.)

7. Place the Pan Lining Paper containing the five tortillas on a 12 x 17-inch cookie sheet.

8. Bake for 12 to 15 minutes. While baking, form the remaining five tortillas.

9. Remove from the oven and place the tortillas on a cooling rack.

10. Bake and cool the remaining tortillas as above.

11. Store in a sealed container in the refrigerator.

Mustard with Red Pepper Flakes Tortillas

MAKES 4 (6-INCH) TORTILLAS

Hot and wild! Perfect as a sandwich wrap, or just a holder for a hot dog.

WET INGREDIENTS

6 tablespoons cold water

1 tablespoon rice vinegar

DRY INGREDIENTS

3 tablespoons mustard powder

½ teaspoon red pepper flakes

½ teaspoon sea salt

1 teaspoon unflavored gelatin

½ cup chia seed meal

1. In a medium bowl, whisk the mustard powder with the cold water. Wait 10 minutes.

2. After 10 minutes, add the vinegar, red pepper flakes, salt, and chia seed meal. Whisk until the mixture becomes doughlike.

3. Place in a container with a lid and refrigerate for 4 hours, or overnight.

4. Place the chilled dough in a large bowl and fold in the gelatin with your preferred utensil. I use a fork.

5. Preheat the oven to 325°F.

6. Form the dough into four tortillas. (See Introduction to Tortillas, page 105.)

7. Place the Pan Lining Paper containing the four tortillas on a 12 x 17-inch cookie sheet.

8. Bake for 12 to 15 minutes.

9. Place the cookie sheet on a hot pad while you turn each tortilla over by carefully lifting it from the parchment before turning it over and placing it back down.

10. Bake for another 5 minutes. Remove from the oven and place the tortillas on a cooling rack.

11. Store in a sealed container in the refrigerator.

Onion Garlic Tortillas

MAKES 8 (6-INCH) TORTILLAS

Awaken your tastebuds with the classic spicy flavors of onion and garlic!
Enhances everyday meals you will want to repeat time after time.

WET INGREDIENTS

2 cups chopped yellow onion

5 garlic cloves

DRY INGREDIENTS

½ teaspoon sea salt

1 cup chia seed meal

2 teaspoons unflavored gelatin

1. In a blender, blend the onion, garlic, and salt thoroughly.

2. Transfer to a medium bowl. Whisk in chia seed meal until the mixture becomes doughlike.

3. Place in a container with a lid and refrigerate for 4 hours, or overnight.

4. Place the chilled dough in a large bowl and fold in the gelatin with your preferred utensil. I use a fork.

5. Preheat the oven to 325°F.

6. Form half of the dough into four tortillas. (See Introduction to Tortillas, page 105.)

7. Place the Pan Lining Paper containing the four tortillas on a 12 x 17-inch cookie sheet.

8. Bake for 12 to 15 minutes. While baking, form the remaining four tortillas.

9. Place the cookie sheet on a hot pad while you turn each tortilla over by carefully lifting it from the parchment before turning it over and placing it back down.

10. Bake for another 5 minutes. Remove from the oven and place the tortillas on a cooling rack.

11. Bake and cool the remaining four tortillas as above.

12. Store in a sealed container in the refrigerator.

Strawberry Vinaigrette Kale Tortillas

MAKES 10 (6-INCH) TORTILLAS

Inspired by healthy salads, these tortillas are perfect for sandwich wraps and crunchy taco salad bowls.

WET INGREDIENTS

11 cups fresh baby kale leaves or chopped curly kale (5-6 ounces)

1 cup chopped fresh strawberries

2 tablespoons raspberry vinegar

DRY INGREDIENTS

½ teaspoon sea salt

1¼ cup chia seed meal

2½ teaspoons unflavored gelatin

1. In a blender, blend the kale, strawberries, salt, and vinegar thoroughly.

2. Transfer to a medium bowl. Whisk in the chia seed meal until the mixture becomes doughlike.

3. Place in a container with a lid and refrigerate for 4 hours, or overnight.

4. Place the chilled dough in a large bowl and fold in the gelatin with your preferred utensil. I use a fork.

5. Preheat the oven to 325°F.

6. Form half of the dough into five tortillas. (See Introduction to Tortillas, page 105.)

7. Place the Pan Lining Paper containing the five tortillas on a 12 x 17-inch cookie sheet before placing in the oven.

8. Bake for 12 to 15 minutes. While baking, form the remaining five tortillas.

9. Place the cookie sheet on a hot pad while you turn each tortilla over by carefully lifting it from the parchment before turning it over and placing it back down.

10. Bake for another 5 minutes. Remove from the oven and place the tortillas on a cooling rack.

11. Bake and cool the remaining five tortillas as above.

12. Store in a sealed container in the refrigerator.

COOKIES, CAKES & BARS

Classic Almond Cookies

MAKES 20 TO 60 COOKIES

A simple recipe made with almond meal, raisins, eggs, and love. A unique and healthy item for your potluck, office party, or fund-raiser!

DRY INGREDIENTS

2 cups almond meal

½ teaspoon baking powder

½ teaspoon sea salt

⅛ teaspoon pure stevia powder (optional)

WET INGREDIENTS

½ cup golden raisins

1 large egg

2 tablespoons olive oil

1½ teaspoons vanilla extract

1. Preheat the oven to 350°F.

2. Cover a 12 x 17-inch cookie sheet with parchment paper.

3. Place the almond meal and raisins in a food processor and pulse until the mixture forms a paste. Then add the remaining ingredients and pulse until mixed.

4. Use a scoop or form the paste by hand into balls. Place on the prepared cookie sheet, evenly spaced with little space between the balls as they don't expand much.

5. Bake for 10 minutes.

6. Let cool on the pan before eating. Store in a sealed container in the refrigerator.

Basic Date Bars

MAKES 10 (4 X 1-INCH) BARS

Simple and delicate for snacks or eating on the run!
These unbaked bars are less sticky than other date bars, and can be made nut free
by using sunflower seed meal or pumpkin seed meal.

DRY INGREDIENTS

3 cups almond meal, (sunflower seed meal, or pumpkin seed meal)

WET INGREDIENTS

3 cups whole pitted dates (12 ounces)

¼ cup lemon juice concentrate

2 tablespoons water

1. Toast the almond meal by placing it on 12 x 17-inch foil-lined baking sheet. Bake at 350°F for 12 to 15 minutes.

2. In a blender, combine the dates, lemon juice concentrate, and water. Start on low speed, then work up to high speed to turn the dates into a smooth paste.

3. Transfer the date paste to a large bowl, then add the toasted almond meal. Blend well.

4. Transfer mixture to 15-inch square of Pan Lining Paper, parchment side up.

5. Place another 15-inch square of Pan Lining Paper on top of dough, parchment side down. Press down on the paper and mold the mixture with your hands through the paper. Use a rolling pin to level to a 1-inch thickness, until 8 x 5 inches. Shape with your fingers and hands into a straight-edged rectangle, switching back and forth from using a rolling pin and your hands as needed.

6. Remove the top paper. Fold the remaining bottom paper over the dough and store in the refrigerator overnight.

7. Remove from the refrigerator and cut into 4 x 1-inch bars with a pizza cutter. Store in the refrigerator.

Black Tea and Fig Bites

MAKES 30 TO 45 COOKIES, DEPENDING ON THE SCOOPING TOOL

A crunchy fig treat with a slight bitter taste of black tea offset by
the sweetness of the figs. An eyebrow-raising addition for any get-together.
Classic flavors combine to delight.

DRY INGREDIENTS

2 teaspoons organic black tea (loose or from 2 tea bags)

2 cups raw, shell-free hemp seeds

1 teaspoon baking powder

½ teaspoon sea salt

WET INGREDIENTS

1½ cups whole dried Mission figs (about 12 whole figs)

½ cup liquid egg whites

1 teaspoon lemon zest

1. Preheat the oven to 375°F.

2. Cover a 12 x 17-inch baking sheet with parchment paper.

3. Remove stems from dried figs then combine all the ingredients in a blender or food processor. Start on low speed. As the whole figs break down into smaller pieces, raise to a higher speed to break them down further.

4. Transfer the mixture to a small mixing bowl.

5. Gently spoon drop bite-size portions of dough 1 inch apart onto the prepared baking sheet. Do not overcompress; keep them loose, pushing the mixture off the spoon with your finger.

6. Bake for 8 to 12 minutes.

7. Allow to cool on the pan. The cookies will harden as they cool. Store in a sealed container in the refrigerator.

Zesty Cranberry Pumpkin Seed Cookies

MAKES 20 TO 30 (2-INCH) COOKIES

Similar to the cracker with same name, this cookie is naturally sweet, thick and soft.
A holiday favorite made from red and green ingredients.

DRY INGREDIENTS

2 cups raw, shell-free pumpkin seeds

1 teaspoon sea salt

WET INGREDIENTS

6 tablespoons water

½ cup dried cranberries

2 teaspoons packed orange zest

1. Preheat the oven to 300°F.

2. Grind the pumpkin seeds into a fine meal.

3. In a small bowl, combine the pumpkin seed meal, water, orange zest, and salt. Mix well until the mixture comes together into a ball.

4. Tear two sheets of Pan Lining Paper big enough to cover a 12 x 17-inch cookie sheet.

5. Place the dough between the two sheets with the parchment sides touching the dough. Roll the dough between the two sheets with a rolling pin until ¼ inch thick.

6. Peel away the top paper gently and reinforce the edges of dough. Some outer edges of the rolled dough may look thinner. Use a rubber spatula to push all the thin edges toward the center of the dough. Smooth the edges with the spatula or reapply the top paper and gently press the edges with your hands. This step helps prevent the outer cookies from having burnt edges. Score the dough into squares. Press firmly with a pizza cutter.

7. Chop the dried cranberries into pieces and sprinkle them across the top. Place parchment paper back on top, and press gently to embed the cranberries in the dough.

8. Slide the bottom paper, with its dough, onto a 12 x 17-inch cookie sheet.

9. Bake for 35 minutes.

10. Let cool for 30 minutes on the pan, then break apart by hand. Store in a sealed container in the refrigerator.

OMG (Oh My Gosh!) Cookies

MAKES 30 TO 50 COOKIES, DEPENDING ON THE SCOOPING TOOL

A combination of crunchy and soft textures satisfies most. After each bite you taste sweet and salty, which is rich and satisfying. Next, a latent touch of warmth slowly unfolds in your mouth. Made from dates and unsweetened coconut shavings, these cookies cause many to exclaim, "Oh my gosh!"

DRY INGREDIENTS

2 teaspoons baking powder

2 teaspoons sea salt

¼ teaspoon cayenne pepper

WET INGREDIENTS

2 cups unsweetened coconut flakes (not shredded coconut)

3 cups whole pitted dates (12 ounces whole dates)

½ cup plus 2 tablespoons liquid egg whites, divided

1. Preheat the oven to 325°F.

2. Cover a 12 x 17-inch baking sheet with parchment paper.

3. Place the 2 tablespoons of liquid egg whites in a small, shallow container and set aside.

4. Combine the remaining ingredients in a blender or a food processor. Your goal is to break down dates and coconut flakes into smaller pieces, not a paste. Start on low speed and raise to a higher speed to break them down further.

5. Transfer the mixture to a small bowl.

6. Dip a teaspoon, ½-inch cookie scoop, or small melon baller into the reserved liquid egg whites to wet it. This will prevent some sticking and will make the cookies crisp. Gently scoop a small amount of the mixture onto the prepared pan, using the wetted scoop. Do not overpress your scoops; keep them gentle. The edges of the dough will be jagged with coconut pieces—this is good. Push the mixture off the spoon with your finger. The melon baller can be tapped on the baking sheet and the mixture will fall out Place the scoops of dough 1 inch apart.

7. Bake for 15 to 20 minutes.

8. Let cool on the pan. The cookies will harden as they cool. Store in a sealed container in the refrigerator.

Peanut Butter Cookies

MAKES ABOUT 24 COOKIES

These peanut butter cookies are crunchy and grain free! Made from whole roasted peanuts, they are packed with flavor and use less sugar too!

DRY INGREDIENTS

1 cup whole raw, shell-free peanuts (see note)

⅓ cup cane sugar

¾ teaspoon baking powder

1 teaspoon sea salt

NOTE: For softer cookies made without whole peanuts, use a total of 1¼ cups peanut butter in recipe.

WET INGREDIENTS

¼ cup peanut butter

¼ cup plus 2 tablespoons liquid egg whites, divided

1. Toast the raw peanuts by placing them on 12 x 17-inch foil-lined baking sheet. Bake at 350°F for 15 minutes. Remove from the oven and let cool.

2. Preheat the oven to 375°F.

3. Grind the cooled, toasted peanuts into a medium meal, using a coffee/spice grinder, or food processor.

4. In a medium bowl, combine the peanut meal, cane sugar, baking powder, and salt. Mix well. Next, add the peanut butter and the ¼ cup of egg whites. Mix well.

5. Spoon drop small amounts of dough onto a parchment-lined 12 x 17-inch cookie sheet. Place the spoonfuls 1 inch apart.

6. Place the remaining 2 tablespoons of egg whites in a small, shallow container.

7. Press crisscross imprints on top with an egg-covered fork. Reinforce the sides of each cookie with your fingers as needed when pressing. Rocking the fork will lengthen your imprints and loosen the fork from the dough. If any dough remains on the fork, wipe it clean before imprinting the next cookie. Rewet the fork with egg whites before pressing each imprint.

8. Bake for 15 minutes. Note: If replacing ground peanuts with peanut butter, reduce the bake time to 10 minutes.

9. Let cool on the pan. Store in a sealed container.

Sunflower Seed Butter Cookies

MAKES 12 TO 15 (1½- TO 2-INCH) COOKIES

Made with ground sunflower seeds, these cookies taste similar to those made from
peanut butter and crumble like traditional cookies, with an aroma of lemon and vanilla.
You can use any variety of sunflower seed butter you find, or grind your own.

DRY INGREDIENTS

1 cup garbanzo bean flour

½ teaspoon pure stevia powder

1 teaspoon baking powder

½ teaspoon sea salt

WET INGREDIENTS

⅛ cup plus 2 tablespoons liquid egg whites, divided

2 teaspoons vanilla extract

¾ teaspoon pure lemon oil (not extract)

¼ cup sunflower seed butter

1. Preheat the oven to 350°F.

2. Line a 12 x 17-inch baking sheet with parchment paper.

3. In a medium bowl, combine the dry ingredients.

4. In a separate bowl, combine 2 tablespoons of the egg whites, vanilla, and lemon oil. Mix well.

5. Now add the sunflower seed butter and the egg white mixture to the bowl of dry ingredients. Mash with a fork until the dough is well mixed and has formed into small, loose pieces.

6. Pinch an amount with your fingers and place in your other hand, then squeeze, making a fist. The pieces will stick together as you continue to squeeze and shape them into flattish ovals 1½ to 2 inches wide. Do not try to roll them into a ball, as they will fall apart. Place 1 inch apart on the prepared baking sheet.

7. Place the remaining 2 tablespoons of egg whites in a small, shallow container. Using a fork, first dip it into the egg whites and then use it to press crisscross imprints on each cookie. Wipe it clean and rewet it every time.

8. Bake for 25 minutes. Let cool on the pan. Store in a sealed container.

Fig Hempie Cookies

MAKES 30 TO 50 COOKIES, DEPENDING ON THE SCOOPING TOOL

Their taste and texture is very similar to classic Fig Newtons, but fig hempies are grain free, gluten free, and sugar free. A great cookie snack that will keep you satisfied all day long. Made from dried Mission figs and hemp seeds, these little cookies are great for travel. Don't forget to share with friends over tea.

DRY INGREDIENTS

1 cup raw, shell-free hemp seeds

1 teaspoon baking powder

½ teaspoon sea salt

WET INGREDIENTS

¼ cup plus 2 tablespoons liquid egg whites, divided

1½ cups whole dried Mission figs (about 8 ounces)

2 teaspoons vanilla extract

1. Preheat the oven to 325°F.

2. Cover a 12 x 17-inch baking sheet with parchment paper.

3. Place the 2 tablespoons of liquid egg whites in a small, shallow bowl and set aside.

4. Remove stems from dried figs then combine all the remaining ingredients in a blender or food processor. Start on low speed. As the whole figs break down into smaller pieces, raise to a higher speed to break them down further.

5. Transfer the fig mixture to a small bowl.

6. Dip a teaspoon, ½-inch cookie scoop, or small melon baller into the reserved liquid egg whites to wet it. This will prevent some sticking and will make the cookies crisp. Gently scoop a small amount of the mixture onto the prepared pan, using the wetted scoop. Do not overpress your scoops; keep them gentle. Push the mixture off the spoon with your finger. The melon baller can be tapped on the baking sheet and the mixture will fall out. Place the scoops 1 inch apart.

7. Bake for 15 to 20 minutes.

8. Let cool on the pan. The cookies will harden as they cool. Store in a sealed container in the refrigerator.

Date Hempie Cookies

Uses dates instead of figs like in the Fig Hempie Cookie. Utilizing dates creates a texture very much like that of a crunchy cookie made from flour.

DRY INGREDIENTS

1 cup raw, shell-free hemp seeds

1 teaspoon baking powder

½ teaspoon sea salt

WET INGREDIENTS

¼ cup plus 2 tablespoons liquid egg whites, divided

1½ cups whole pitted dates (6 ounces whole dates)

2 teaspoons vanilla extract

1. Preheat the oven to 325°F.

2. Cover a 12 x 17-inch baking sheet with parchment paper.

3. Place the 2 tablespoons of egg whites in a small, shallow container. Set aside.

4. Combine all the remaining ingredients in a blender or food processor. Start on low speed. As the whole dates break down into smaller pieces, raise to a higher speed to break them down further.

5. Transfer the date mixture to a small mixing bowl.

6. Dip a teaspoon or small melon baller into the reserved liquid egg whites to wet it. This will prevent some sticking and will keep the cookies crisp. Gently scoop a small amount of the mixture onto the prepared pan, using the wetted scoop. Do not overpress your scoops; keep them gentle. Push the mixture off the spoon with your finger. The melon baller can be tapped on the baking sheet and the mixture will fall out. Place the scoops about 1 inch apart.

7. Bake for 15 to 20 minutes.

8. Let cool on the pan. The cookies will harden as they cool. Store in a sealed container in the refrigerator.

Pumpkin Seed with Ginger Cookies

MAKES 20 TO 60 COOKIES

Use pumpkin seeds instead of almonds in the classic almond cookie. Perfect for fall and winter holidays. These ginger cookies are grain free, nut free, and sweetened with fruit. A tasty option to accompany tea, coffee, hot chocolate, or milk.

DRY INGREDIENTS

2 cups raw, shell-free pumpkin seeds

1½ teaspoons ground ginger

½ teaspoon baking powder

½ teaspoon sea salt

¼ teaspoon pure stevia powder (optional)

WET INGREDIENTS

½ cup golden raisins

1 large egg

2 tablespoons olive oil

1. Preheat the oven to 350°F.

2. Cover a 12 x 17-inch cookie sheet with parchment paper.

3. Place the pumpkin seeds and raisins in a food processor and pulse until the mixture forms a paste. Then add the remaining ingredients and pulse until mixed.

4. Form the paste into 1-inch balls. Place on the prepared cookie sheet, evenly spaced with little space between the balls as they don't expand much.

5. Bake for 10 minutes.

6. Let cool on the pan before eating. Store in a sealed container in the refrigerator.

Apricot with Lime Cookies

MAKES 30 TO 60 COOKIES, DEPENDING ON THE SCOOPING TOOL

Small in bite but pleasing to lovers of apricots and cookies. Chewy, crunchy, and delicious makes true tropical delight.

DRY INGREDIENTS

2 teaspoons baking powder

½ teaspoon sea salt

WET INGREDIENTS

½ cup plus 2 tablespoons liquid egg whites, divided

2 cups unsweetened coconut flakes (not shredded coconut)

2 cups dried apricots

4 teaspoons lime zest

1. Preheat the oven to 325°F.

2. Cover a 12 x 17-inch baking sheet with parchment paper.

3. Place the 2 tablespoons of the liquid egg whites in a small, shallow container.

4. Combine all the remaining ingredients in a blender or a food processor. Your goal is break the apricots and coconut flakes down into smaller pieces, not a paste. Start on low speed and raise to a higher speed to break them down further.

5. Transfer the mixture to a small bowl.

6. Dip a teaspoon, ½-inch cookie scoop, or small melon baller into the reserved liquid egg whites to wet it. This will prevent some sticking and will make the cookies crisp. Gently scoop a small amount of the mixture onto the prepared pan, using the wetted scoop. Do not overpress your scoops; keep them gentle. The edges of the dough will be jagged with coconut pieces—this is good. Push the mixture off the spoon with your finger. The melon baller can be tapped on the baking sheet and the mixture will fall out. Place the scoops 1 inch apart.

7. Bake for 15 to 20 minutes.

8. Let cool on the pan. The cookies will harden as they cool. Store in a sealed container in the refrigerator.

Black Bean Brownies

MAKES 8 WEDGES

A rich, dark chocolate brownie made with cocoa powder and coconut oil.
This brownie is black bean based, but tastes like pure chocolate. The dense, moist
center and light, cakelike top hide its grain-free secret very well.
Feel free to mix it up by replacing the coconut oil with real butter, or even banana.

DRY INGREDIENTS

¾ cup cane sugar

⅛ teaspoon pure stevia powder (optional)

¼ teaspoon sea salt

1 cup unsweetened cocoa powder

⅛ teaspoon baking soda

¼ teaspoon baking powder

WET INGREDIENTS

1¼ cups cooked black beans, or 1 (15-ounce) can, drained and rinsed

2 large eggs

⅔ cup solid coconut oil

2 tablespoons vanilla extract

1. Preheat the oven to 350°F.

2. Lightly grease an 8½-inch pie pan.

3. In a blender, combine the beans, eggs, coconut oil, cane sugar, stevia powder (optional), vanilla, and salt.

4. Sift the cocoa powder over a medium bowl. Mix in the baking soda and baking powder.

5. Transfer the black bean mixture to the bowl of dry ingredients and mix thoroughly.

6. Use a spatula to transfer the batter into the prepared pan.

7. Bake for 30 minutes.

8. Serve immediately or let cool. Slice like a pie. Store in the refrigerator.

Blondies

A cocoa-free brownie made with pure cane sugar. This brownie is flour free and does not skimp on its rich, sweet flavor. Dense and moist with a light, cakelike quality. Feel free to substitute sunflower seed meal for the almond meal. You can even replace the coconut oil with real butter or banana.

DRY INGREDIENTS

1½ cups almond meal

1 teaspoon baking powder

⅛ teaspoon pure stevia powder (optional)

¼ teaspoon sea salt

¾ cup cane sugar

WET INGREDIENTS

1¼ cups cooked Great Northern beans, or 1 (15.8-ounce) can, drained and rinsed

½ cup liquid egg whites

⅓ cup solid coconut oil

2 tablespoons vanilla extract

1. Preheat the oven to 350°F.

2. Lightly grease an 8½-inch pie pan.

3. Place the almond meal, baking powder, stevia powder (optional), and salt in a medium bowl. Mix well. Set aside.

4. In a blender, combine the beans, egg whites, coconut oil, cane sugar, and vanilla. Blend very well for 1 minute.

5. Transfer the bean mixture to the bowl of dry ingredients and mix thoroughly.

6. Use a spatula to transfer the batter into the prepared pan.

7. Bake for 30 minutes, or until the blondies start to brown on top.

8. Serve immediately or let cool. Slice like a pie. Store in the refrigerator.

Mesquite Pod Brownies

MAKES 8 WEDGES

Cocoa-sensitive persons cannot eat chocolate, but they can enjoy this chocolatey
delight, made with mesquite pod flour instead of cocoa. Low sugar,
oil free, flour free, this brownie is dense, moist, and dark. The taste is
so close to real chocolate it will fool most.

DRY INGREDIENTS

1½ cups mesquite pod
flour (1 [8 ounce] package)

1 teaspoon baking powder

⅛ teaspoon pure stevia
powder (optional)

¼ teaspoon sea salt

½ cup cane sugar

WET INGREDIENTS

1¼ cups cooked Great
Northern beans, or
1 (15.8-ounce) can,
drained and rinsed

2 large eggs

2 tablespoons vanilla
extract

1. Preheat the oven to 350°F.

2. Lightly grease an 8½-inch pie pan.

3. Sift the mesquite pod flour gently and close to the
bottom of a medium bowl because this flour is very
fine and will get in the air.

4. Add the baking powder, stevia powder (optional),
and salt. Mix well. Set aside.

5. In a blender, combine the beans, eggs, cane sugar,
and vanilla. Blend very well for 1 minute.

6. Transfer the bean mixture to the bowl of dry ingredients and mix slowly and gently until well mixed.

7. Use a spatula to transfer the batter into the prepared
pan.

8. Bake for 30 minutes.

9. Let cool. Best after sitting covered at room tem-
perature for 12 hours. Slice like a pie. Store in the
refrigerator.

Chocolate Cake

MAKES ONE 9-INCH CAKE

This chocolate cake recipe is flour free, gluten free, and nut free. An amazingly tasty, simple, and healthy recipe.

DRY INGREDIENTS

1 cup cocoa powder

½ teaspoon baking soda

1 teaspoon baking powder

1 cup cane sugar

¼ teaspoon pure stevia powder

½ teaspoon sea salt

WET INGREDIENTS

2½ cups cooked black beans, or 2 (15-ounce) cans, drained and rinsed

4 large eggs

⅔ cup solid coconut oil

4 tablespoons vanilla extract

1. Preheat the oven to 350°F.

2. Lightly grease 9-inch round cake pan.

3. In a medium bowl, combine the cocoa powder, baking soda, and baking powder. Stir well. Set aside.

4. In a blender, combine the beans, eggs, coconut oil, cane sugar, stevia powder, vanilla, and salt. Blend well.

5. Transfer the bean mixture to the bowl of dry ingredients and mix thoroughly.

6. Pour the batter into the prepared pan.

7. Bake for 35 minutes.

8. Let cool in the pan. Store in the refrigerator.

Cocoa Microwave Mug Cake

SERVES 1

A dark chocolate cake with natural specks of blue. Eat plain or dress up with fruit and icing. Perfect for celebrating yourself or others.

DRY INGREDIENTS

¾ cup almond meal (see note #1)

3 tablespoons cocoa powder

½ teaspoon baking powder

2 tablespoons cane sugar (optional) (see note #2)

WET INGREDIENTS

½ cup liquid egg whites

½ cup fresh blueberries

2 teaspoons vanilla extract

1. In a 20-ounce microwave-proof mug or bowl, stir together the almond meal, cocoa powder, baking powder, and cane sugar (optional).

2. Combine the egg whites, blueberries, and vanilla in a single-serve blender or immersion stick blender with mixing cup. Blend well.

3. Transfer the blueberry mixture to the mug of dry ingredients and mix well.

4. Microwave on high for 3 minutes.

5. Let sit for 5 minutes. Serve in the bowl, or remove to add icing or decorations.

6. Serve warm in mug, or remove to decorate.

NOTE #1: To make recipe nut-free grind ¾ cup raw shell-free sunflower seeds into a fine meal to replace almond meal.
NOTE #2: Make without sugar for a plain cocoa bread perfect for butters and sweet spreads.

Banana Microwave Mug Cake

SERVES 1

A fast version of the traditional banana bread but without the need for any sugar.

DRY INGREDIENTS

¾ cup almond meal (see note)

¼ cup golden flaxseed meal

½ teaspoon baking powder

WET INGREDIENTS

10 whole pitted dried dates

⅓ cup liquid egg whites

⅓ cup mashed ripe banana

1. In a 20-ounce microwave-proof mug or bowl, stir together the almond meal, flaxseed meal, and baking powder.

2. Chop dates into smaller pieces.

3. Using a single-serve or immersion stick blender, combine the dates, egg whites, and banana.

4. Transfer the fruit mixture to the bowl of dry ingredients and mix well.

5. Microwave on high for 3 minutes.

6. Let sit for 5 minutes. Serve in the bowl, or remove to add icing or decorations.

7. Serve warm, or let cool. Store in a sealed container in the refrigerator.

NOTE: To make recipe nut-free, grind ¾ cup raw shell-free sunflower seeds into a fine meal to replace almond meal.

Pumpkin Microwave Mug Cake

SERVES 1

Tastes like pumpkin pie, but in a cake form. Sugar is minimal and optional.

DRY INGREDIENTS

¾ cup almond meal (see note)

1 teaspoon pumpkin pie spice

1 teaspoon baking powder

1 tablespoon cane sugar (optional)

WET INGREDIENTS

½ cup liquid egg whites

⅓ cup canned pure pumpkin

1. In a 20-ounce or larger microwave-proof mug or bowl, stir together the almond meal, pumpkin pie spice, baking powder, and sugar (optional).

2. Using a single-serve or immersion stick blender, blend together well the egg whites and pumpkin.

3. Transfer the pumpkin mixture to the bowl of dry ingredients and mix well.

4. Microwave on high for 3 minutes.

5. Let sit for 5 minutes. Serve in the bowl, or remove to add icing or decorations.

6. Serve warm, or let cool. Store in a sealed container in the refrigerator.

NOTE: To make recipe nut-free, grind ¾ cup raw shell-free sunflower seeds into a fine meal to replace almond meal.

Carrot Microwave Mug Cake

SERVES 1

A unique twist on carrot cake. Pine nuts and nutmeg each contribute their own flair.

DRY INGREDIENTS

¼ cup pine nuts

¾ cup almond meal (see note)

1 teaspoon baking powder

Pinch of ground nutmeg (¹⁄₁₆ teaspoon)

1 tablespoon cane sugar (optional)

WET INGREDIENTS

½ cup liquid egg whites

½ cup finely grated carrot

1 teaspoon lemon zest

1 teaspoon vanilla extract

1. Toast the pine nuts by placing in a small, dry skillet over medium-high heat. Move the pan back and forth about every 30 seconds to prevent the nuts from burning. When the nuts are sufficiently toasted, transfer to a small, heatproof container. The nuts will continue to roast in their own heat. Let cool.

2. In a small cup, combine the grated carrot, lemon zest, and vanilla.

3. Grind, but just briefly, the cooled, toasted pine nuts in a coffee/spice grinder.

4. In a 20-ounce microwave-proof mug or bowl, stir together the almond meal, toasted pine nut bits, baking powder, nutmeg, and cane sugar, if using.

5. Transfer the carrot mixture and egg whites to the bowl of dry ingredients, and mix well by hand.

6. Microwave on high for 3 minutes.

7. Let sit for 5 minutes. Serve in the bowl, or remove to add icing or decorations.

8. Serve warm, or let cool. Store in a sealed container in the refrigerator.

NOTE: To make recipe nut-free, grind ¾ cup raw shell-free sunflower seeds into a fine meal to replace almond meal.

Mistaken for Baked Cheesecake

MAKES ONE 8½-INCH CAKE

If you've ever wanted a dairy-free, soy-free, and crust-free cheesecake, then you've found it! Extremely rich and flavorful, with the same texture and flavors as the real deal. This delightful dessert is sure to please most.

DRY INGREDIENTS

2 cups whole raw macadamia nuts (8 ounces)

⅛ teaspoon pure stevia powder (optional)

1 teaspoon baking powder

¾ cup cane sugar

¼ teaspoon sea salt

WET INGREDIENTS

1¼ cups cooked Great Northern beans, or 1 (15.8-ounce) can, drained and rinsed

½ cup liquid egg whites

2 tablespoons vanilla extract

⅓ cup solid coconut oil

2 teaspoons lemon zest

1. Preheat the oven to 350°F.

2. Lightly grease an 8½-inch pie pan.

3. In a blender, combine the beans, egg whites, vanilla, coconut oil, and macadamia nuts. Blend well. The mixture will be very thick.

4. Transfer the mixture to a large bowl and use whisk to thoroughly mix in the lemon zest, baking powder, cane sugar, salt, and stevia (optional).

5. Use a spatula to transfer the batter into the prepared pie pan.

6. Bake for 30 minutes.

7. Let cool. Store in the refrigerator.

APPENDIX

Here are the published instructions that kick-started the revolution:

Make Breads and Crackers Using Only Veggies and Seeds

Is there such a thing as a veggie flour?

No, but you can make veggie-only breads and crackers by adding a secret ingredient used by raw food chefs that makes nonstarchy ingredients stick together the way flour does (a trick I was taught by raw cracker expert Krazy Kracker Lady). Now, even regular folk, with the help of an oven, can make healthy veggie flatbreads and crackers!

Just follow this basic veggie bread recipe:

First, grind your favorite raw veggies into a thick liquid, using a blender. Using the measuring indicators on the side, continue adding veggies until the contents measure 3 cups. Consider adding a tomato or water to make sure all the veggies are blended well. If you need to, lightly steam your veggies first before adding to the blender.

Second, you'll need 1½ cups of finely ground flax, or chia seeds. These seeds get sticky when wet and will turn your wet veggies doughy. To grind whole seeds, use a clean coffee grinder or a single-serve blender with a dry blade.

In a bowl, mix together thoroughly the liquid veggies and finely ground seeds. Add seasonings and salt if you want. Let the mixture sit for 10 minutes. Pour a little high-heat-tolerant oil, such as sunflower, avocado, or coconut oil, onto a 9 x 13-inch cookie sheet. Press the mixture by hand to cover the baking sheet evenly. Bake in a preheated 350°F oven for 45 minutes to 1 hour. This makes a tasty unleavened flatbread that's firm on the outside and moist in the middle. To make crackers instead, split the mixture over two cookie sheets, and cut the bake time in half.

This great alternative bread and cracker recipe can be used for sandwiches, pizza dough, snacks, side dishes, or even breakfast on the go. The flavoring options are endless and the health benefits of eating a veggie-dense food are priceless.

Now, even food allergy/sensitive people can eat great "bread" without carbs, nuts, gluten, or guilt!

*Adapted from *Austin All Natural Magazine,* July 2012, 17.

ACKNOWLEDGMENTS

I would like to publicly thank my friends who helped me in the kitchen. Tula Robbins and I share a love for healthy alternative food and nutrition. I enjoy her help, conversations and friendship. Kathleen Elkins took on the task of kitchen help via her excitement for the project in support of me and our friendship that stretches back a decade, and I am deeply grateful. Cynthia Harrell devoted months in the kitchen beside me and was reliable, supportive, and never lost excitement for any recipe—even the one I asked her to bake over eleven times in my relentless pursuit of perfection—Cynthia is herself also a form of perfection.

Thank you to my husband, Joe Vitale, who was the instigator of this project and who never let me lose sight of those who need this book, and how their lives could be helped. He made space for this project in our house and supported this project in many ways including always enjoying all the vegetables in my breads.

Special mentions of support and encouragement go to Michael Abedin, Victoria Schaefer, Rick and Mary Barrett, Matt Holt, Jessica Guiterrez-Koons, Mary Rose Lam, Suzanne Burns, Lisa Daidone, my mother Dorothy Carroll, Michele Eilers, Deana Dossey, Kristin J. Starr, Maria and Bill Phillips, Bruce and Hollie Collie and the Collie Clan, Mathew and Shannon Dixon, Casey Whitaker, Shelly Lefkoe, Robin Jeambert, Susan and Perry Raybuck, Mendhi Audlin, Bruce Grether, Tom Manes, Daniel and Andrea Barrett, Laura Fleming-Holcomb, Rita H. Losee, my agent Marilyn Allen, and Ann Treistman and The Countryman Press.

INDEX

* Note: Page references in *italics* indicate recipe photographs.

Mushrooms
    Garlic Buttered Mushroom Loaf, 62, *63*
    Mushroom Biscuits, *94*, 95
Mustard with Red Pepper Flakes Tortillas, *120*, 121

N

Non-stick baking liner, 22
Nuts. *See* Macadamia nuts; Peanuts; Pecans; Pine nuts

O

Okra
    Southwestern Okra Bread, 38
    Soy Nut Okra Muffins, *80*, 81
    Texas Traditional Okra Bread, 43
Onions
    Garlic Onion Bread, *50*, 51
    Onion Garlic Tortillas, 122
    Ranch Onion Bread, 52
Orange Spice Bread, *74*, 75

P

Paleo breads, 18–19
Paleo diet, 14
Pan Lining Paper, 21, 22
Parchment paper, 22
Parmesan Pepper Zucchini Bread, *66*, 67
Peanut butter
    OMG (Oh My Gosh!) Cookies, *132*, 133
Peanuts
    OMG (Oh My Gosh!) Cookies, *132*, 133
Pecans
    Banana Bread, 68
    Dark Spicy Banana Bread, 69
Peppers. *See* Jalapeño peppers; Red bell peppers; Serrano peppers
Pie pans, 23
Pine nuts
    Carrot Microwave Mug Cake, 154
    Sunflower Zucchini Loaf with Pine Nuts, *60*, 61
    Taste of India Bread, 34

Pinto beans
    Mild Pinto Bean Tortillas, 119
Probiotics, 16
Pumpkin
    Pumpkin Microwave Mug Cake, 153
Pumpkin seed meal, 24
    Basic Date Bars, 128
Pumpkin seeds
    Acorn Squash Biscuits, *90*, 91
    Acorn Squash Bread, *48*, 49
    Asian Kale Bread, 45
    Cactus Bread, 39
    Garlic Pumpkin Crackers, *84*, 85
    Parmesan Pepper Zucchini Bread, *66*, 67
    Pumpkin Seed Crackers, 86
    Pumpkin Seed with Ginger Cookies, 141
    Southern Flame Bread, *36*, 37
    Zesty Cranberry Pumpkin Seed Cookies, 130, *131*
    Zesty Cranberry Pumpkin Seed Crackers, 87

Q

Quick breads, 14, 59–75. *See also* Muffins
    Banana Bread, 68
    Cinnamon Apple Raisin Bread, 70, *71*
    Cranberry, Carrot & Lemon Bread, *64*, 65
    Dark Spicy Banana Bread, 69
    Fresh Sweet Corn Bread, *58*, 59
    Garlic Buttered Mushroom Loaf, 62, *63*
    Lemon Strawberry Bread, *72*, 73
    Orange Spice Bread, *74*, 75
    Parmesan Pepper Zucchini Bread, *66*, 67
    Sunflower Zucchini Loaf with Pine Nuts, *60*, 61

R

Raisins. *See also* Golden raisins
    Cinnamon Apple Raisin Bread, 70, *71*
Ranch Onion Bread, 52

Raw food movement, 14
Red bell peppers
    Asian Kale Bread, 45
    Holy Hotness Bread, *40*, 41
    Southern Flame Bread, *36*, 37
    Soy Nut Okra Muffins, *80*, 81
    Sweet Spicy Corn Muffins, *76*, 77
    Taste of India Bread, 34
Rheumatoid arthritis, 16

S

Sandwich breads, 31–55
    Acorn Squash Bread, *48*, 49
    Asian Kale Bread, 45
    Cactus Bread, 39
    Croutons, *54*, 55
    Garlic Onion Bread, *50*, 51
    Gratitude Herb Bread, 44
    Hippie Chick Bread, *32*, 33
    Holy Hotness Bread, *40*, 41
    Lemon Garlic Spinach Bread, 53
    Lemon Rosemary Squash Bread, *30*, 31
    Ranch Onion Bread, 52
    Southern Flame Bread, *36*, 37
    Southwestern Okra Bread, 38
    Taste of India Bread, 34, *35*
    Texas Traditional Okra Bread, *42*, 43
    Tomato Sauce Bread, 46, *47*
Sausage Cheddar Biscuits, 100
Seeds. *See also* Hemp seeds; Pumpkin seeds; Sunflower seeds
    making with veggies and seeds, 161
Semicarbazide, 15
Serrano peppers
    Cactus Bread, 39
    Holy Hotness Bread, *40*, 41
    Southern Flame Bread, *36*, 37
Southern Flame Bread, *36*, 37
Southwestern Okra Bread, 38
Soy Nut Okra Muffins, *80*, 81
Spatulas, 23
Spice grinders, 22